Budgetary Thought for Budget Officers

A Practitioner's Perspective

Edward Anthony Lehan

Also By The Author

The Practice of Municipal Budgeting - A Self-Instruction Text
Bureau of Governmental Research, University of Rhode Island, 1975

Simplified Governmental Budgeting
Governmental Finance Officers Association, 1981

Budgetary thought for School Officials
Cantabrigia, 1982

Budgetmaking - A Workbook of Public Budgeting Theory and Practice
St, Martin's Press, 1984

© 2015 Edward Anthony Lehan

All rights reserved. Except for brief quotations, no part of this publication may be reproduced, stored in a retrieval system, or transmitted in any form or by any means, electronic, mechanical, photocopying, recording or otherwise, without the prior permission of the copyright owner. Contact data follows:

ISBN: 1503335437
ISBN 13: 9781503335431
Library of Congress Control Number: 2014921069
CreateSpace Independent Publishing Platform
North Charleston, South Carolina

Edward Anthony Lehan
89 Rumford Street
West Hartford, CT 06107
(860) 521-7097
ealehan@att.net

Budgetary Thought for Budget Officers

CONTENTS

Acknowledgements ix

An Introductory Note 1

    I. Key Ideas and Conditioning Factors 3
    II. The Budget Officer 13
    III. The Grammar of Budgeting 33
    IV. Accounting Foundations 67
    V. Formulation and Documentation Guidelines 79
    VI. Preliminary Work 101
    VII. Key Task: Assessing the Merit of Allocations 141
    VIII. Implementation Methodology: Dynamic Monitoring ... 189

A Concluding Note 211

ACKNOWLEDGEMENTS

It is fitting that I acknowledge the debt I owe to three educators, all of fond memory, who decisively influenced my life choices: Bernice Owen, an English teacher at Hall High School, West Hartford, Connecticut; Pascal Poe, Dean, Hillyer College, Hartford, Connecticut; and Karl Bosworth, Professor, Department of Government, University of Connecticut. Each contributed to my intellectual development, and, equally important, provided wise counsel.

Moreover, I was fortunate to work with competent civil servants who provided me with practical experience and guidance in the craft of public administration and public budgeting: Robert Duffy, several times a finance director; Bernard A. Batycki, a quintessential public executive; and Elisha C. Freedman, city manager, par excellence.

Further, only authors know what they owe to their reviewers. The following acknowledgements attest to the depth of my debt to three reviewers, each an experienced budget officer: Joseph T. Kelley, finance director, lecturer and author; Patricia Cameron, long a key budget officer of the Government of Jamaica; and Ted Zaleski III, Director of Management and Budget, Carroll Country, Maryland.

A special note of thanks is due to Joe Kelley, who, over the years, never tired of advising me to apply logic and math to budgeting problems.

These reviewers encouraged me to complete the manuscript, and provided me with valuable insights concerning its form and substance. More than they know, this trio of reviewers, each reflecting unique experience and talent, helped me to perfect this book.

Budgetary Thought for Budget Officers

Finally, I dedicate this book to Myron E. Weiner, scholar, teacher and author. For more time than either of us care to count, he has been a source of encouragement and intellectual stimulation. His thinking and teaching about administrative behavior influenced me throughout my career, and is reflected throughout the form and substance of this book.

Edward Anthony Lehan

West Hartford, Connecticut
September, 2015

AN INTRODUCTORY NOTE

The evolution of budgeting, and hence, the employment of budget officers, is undoubtedly a response to deep running social currents affecting the organization and activity of contemporary governments. As strategically placed officials, the persona and mentality of budget officers are deeply affected by their daily struggle to help solve a fundamental problem facing the governments they serve:

The necessity to ration scarce resources.

Although thinking focused by the reality of rationing is obviously not confined to budget officers, it certainly is *the* preoccupation of their occupation. As a one-time practitioner, I came to believe that, even though they may be technically qualified by education and experience, budget officers need models of appropriate thinking to condition their conduct, and enhance their effectiveness. Consequently, this book dwells on the intellectual requirements of budget officers, and the associated institutionalized processes which can nourish their minds.

As noted, budget officers owe their occupation to deep-running social currents. Everywhere, contemporary society is distinguished by increasing occupational and personal differentiation. As pointed out by sociologists, differentiation profoundly affects relationships in every sphere of human life — expanding the role and importance of secondary at the expense of primary institutions. Increasingly, modern citizens pursue specialized lives. Economically and socially differentiated, they depend on remote others across the globe for the means of subsistence, and the conveniences and distractions of modern life. Increasingly urbanized, they are abjectly dependent on an infrastructure and public order which makes life possible, and efficient. Although they maintain family ties and practice neighborliness, modern citizens characteristically base intimate relationships on affinity and shared interests, rather than blood and propinquity. Pursuing unique daily agendas, hurrying about on different paths and private schedules, struggling for status, competing for money, power and honor, modern citizens are acutely dependent on government regulation and services. And mark this: As the social controls and services provided by primary institutions, principally the family, weaken, personal insecurity, physical and psychological, increases.

Governments are, by far, the most important of all secondary institutions. Consequently, governments expand to facilitate the satisfaction of private wants and to service public needs. Decades of recent experience demonstrate that the desire and pressure for government regulation and expenditure is persistent and expansive. Further, experience also indicates that measures to provide the resources to satisfy this desire and pressure are resisted. Consequently, at any given time, limited resources must be rationed. The development of budgets and budgeting procedures, and hence, budget offices and budget officers, is traceable to the incongruity between limited resources and limitless desire. Governments employ budget officers to help their accountable officials ration the resources made available to them by the society they serve.

In this book, readers will find that I treat the work of budget officers as a craft, rather than an art requiring virtuosic talent. It is an important distinction because "craftsmanship" implies that the intellectual and practical aspects of budgeting can be codified and the requisite knowledge and skill taught and learned. As appropriate action requires the light of reasoned thought, the title of this book reflects my high regard for the intellectual foundations of budgetary craftsmanship.

I. KEY IDEAS and CONDITIONING FACTORS

Duly adopted by appropriation authorities, government budgets grant designated officials the right to spend public funds, as allocated. These budgets represent a response by political leaders to an absolute need to ration relatively scarce resources. Driven by the hopes and promises of politics, the necessity to ration public resources pits a spectrum of wants and needs against finite means. In effect, the process inclines participating officials and interested parties to think and act in characteristic ways. Because they are preoccupied with budgeting, per se, certain ideas and conditioning factors have special force and affect for budget officers. As noted in the discussion that follows, the *intellectual environment* of budget officers is fundamentally grounded by the following factors:

- The pressure of the rationing requirement, and its practical work-a-day ramifications.

- The prescriptive task to measure and render judgment on 1) the *intrinsic* merit of public programs by applying objective standards of effectiveness, efficiency and economy (the efficacy triad), and 2) their *relative* merit by applying concepts and measurements that reduce the subjectivity of judgment.

Of prime importance, we first note that rationing processes are inherently *conservative*. The endless arguments over getting and spending tell us that participating officials and interested parties are acutely conscious that they are working within a boundary of limited resources. Significantly, a circle is the appropriate image of this fundamental reality. Depending on the fiscal policy of a given government, the circumference of its symbolic circle expands or contracts, as more or less resources are drawn into the budget process from the economic environment. When displayed in budget documentation, circles (known as "pie charts") are segmented by shares, testifying to the inherently *competitive* nature of the rationing process. The shares of these segmented circles are scaled to show the relative size of various programmatic expenditures. Pie charts are also used to graphically present the proportionate contributions of specific revenues to total revenue. Obviously, if budget authorities of a given jurisdiction think that they can expand the circle's circumference by drawing in more resources, they are under less pressure to adjust shares. This ever-present possibility tempts budget authorities to favor budget expansion over programmatic adjustments.

In governments of general jurisdiction, the competitive nature of the rationing process often makes budgeting an uncertain, dramatic process, fraught with surprises. The formulation process encourages expectations. Reflecting on this situation, someone once whimsically said that an equal distribution of dissatisfaction is the criterion of a good budget. The competitive nature of budgeting fosters a general concern that formulation, adoption and implementation procedures should be conducted fairly. All claimants to a portion of the public treasury have an interest in how their claim will be judged. So, *equity* joins conservation and competition as key factors influencing the process of public budgeting, considered as a rationing process. Budget officers are especially concerned with equity, as their recommendations must rest on a deserved reputation for impartial analysis and judgment. Also, as prime custodians of the budget process, budget officers must be ever alert to threats to its integrity, deceptive estimates, for example. Further, the

I. KEY IDEAS and CONDITIONING FACTORS

influence of equity considerations can be clearly seen during times of retrenchment when government leaders order indiscriminate hiring freezes and across-the-board allocation reductions, rather than strive to prioritize allocations.

Viewed historically, government budgets tend to change marginally from year-to- year. However, we must quickly note that, although annual changes may be small, the cumulative effect of compounding over time produces significant change. Consequently, seasoned budget officers are often very reluctant to dismiss small incremental changes. History also provides evidence that budget shares allocated to various programmatic purposes are relatively stable from year-to-year. Clearly, those parties with vested interests in current arrangements have compelling incentives to oppose radical shifts in programmatic allocations. Accordingly, radical shifts tend to occur in "crisis" situations, such as, wars, crime waves, natural disasters, severe economic dislocations, etc. And, it is critically important to note, new patterns, once established, tend to persist as stable allocations.

It has been widely observed that administrative and legislative officials tend to treat the current budget as a "base" for the formulation of next year's budget, rather than as a circumstance deserving serious examination. This conservative tendency strongly conditions the thrust and scope of budgetary reviews, effectively channeling the time and attention of budget officers away from efficacy concerns about the "base" toward the evaluation of proposed incremental changes. Indeed, budget officers who present accountable administrative and legislative officials with unfavorable findings and recommendations concerning the intrinsic or relative merit of established programs are frequently disappointed with their unenthusiastic response.

Nevertheless, budget officers must relentlessly pursue opportunities to displace program goals and/or substitute program procedures. Otherwise public programs, and their procedures, tend to roll on, unchallenged and essentially unchanged, from year-to-year. In the heavily-weighted inertial environment of government bureaucracies, budget officers must aggressively promote the concept of *goal displacement and means substitution.* This is important work, because redirecting allocations from ineffective and/or inefficient programs to new initiatives enables governments to address new problems without additional taxes or loans.

The disposition to relentlessly pursue opportunities for goal displacement and means substitution is a distinguishing mark of competent budget officers.

In his essay, *"Politics as a Vocation,"* the sociologist, Max Weber, described politics as a strong and slow boring of hard boards. Based on my experience, this conceptualization can also be applied to the work of budget officers. Due to the weight of official motivations conditioning the public budgeting process, incremental change is the normal "name of the game." Consequently, budget officers must be patient, but persistent, in expressing the values of the efficacy triad. Such are the vicissitudes of politics that desirable programmatic changes that have no chance of acceptance in one year may get a sympathetic hearing in another.

Despite passive resistance, and disappointing returns on time invested in examining current year expenditure patterns, budget officers are honor-bound to call attention to desirable changes in basic programmatic arrangements when, in their judgment, they are warranted. Consequently, budget officers should view requests for incremental changes as an opportunity to explore the related base. From this perspective, a request for increased resources presents an occasion to inquire into production arrangements, using the concepts and measurements of the efficacy triad as probing instruments. Can enhanced performance ratios be obtained with current production techniques? Or, will requested additional resources change production techniques, enhancing performance ratios? In short, budget officers can profitably pursue the task of evaluating the intrinsic merit of existing

I. KEY IDEAS and CONDITIONING FACTORS

programmatic production arrangements by applying the concepts and measurements of the efficacy triad to proposed incremental expenditures. Further, for future reference, budget officers should relentlessly recommend that results promised by proposed increments be made subject to measurements of effectiveness, efficiency and economy, strictly monitored and reported.

The competitive nature of the process is most strongly felt by officials when they struggle to assess the relative merit of proposed allocations. In a seminal article in the American Political Science Review, "*The Lack of a Budgetary Theory,*" January, 1940, V.O. Key, Jr. discussed the competitive nature of the public budgeting process and the resulting requirement for decision criteria. He summed up the situation with this oft-quoted question: On what basis shall it be decided to allocate X dollars to activity A instead of activity B? Not finding satisfactory criteria, Professor Key suggested that procedures fostering competition among alternatives might be the best approach, forcing the participants in the budget process to rigorously examine their choices.

Certainly, the adoption of tax and expenditure limitations and requirements for balanced budgets intensify competition within a total budget by restricting expansion. The concept of providing parents of public school students with vouchers directing public funds to schools of their choice is calculated to create a competitive environment for education allocations. The "zero-base" approach to public budgets aims at curbing the "inertial" influence of existing arrangements on the future, and requires systematic prioritization of proposed allocations. Although rarely employed, formal weighting and scoring procedures also provide a method requiring participants in the budget process to "objectify" their subjective judgments. These are institutional, rather than analytical, solutions to the generic problem presented by governmental activity: In any given jurisdiction, the subjects and objects of public expenditure are always unique. Lacking common denominators, and easy-to-apply analytical instruments, officials are forced to rely on subjective criteria to make judgments about the relative merit of proposed allocations.

To cope with this ever-present condition, budget officers may apply two analytical instruments which can help reduce the application of subjective criteria in assessing the relative merit of unique programs and projects: 1) marginal productivity comparisons, and 2) benefit/cost comparisons. Both instruments are theoretically sound, but have methodological drawbacks which limit their practical application.

The first technique requires the location of program investment and the measure of its expected results on a so-called "lazy S" curve, popularly known as the curve graphically describing the "law of diminishing returns." (This curve is depicted by Exhibit 7.4, *Marginal Productivity*.) The employment of marginal productivity computations can make percentage changes in productivity measures a common denominator of program-to-program comparisons. Assessing the merit of public expenditure patterns through the lens of marginal productivity tends to show that relationships between applied resources and results are often curvilinear, rather than linear. (Contrast this characteristic with the widely held belief that the relationship between public expenditure and desired results is linear, that is, "the more you spend, the more you get.") The prevalence of curvilinear relationships strongly suggests that governments are likely to be spending too much or too little on given programs. Consequently, applying the concept of marginal productivity to public expenditure patterns can encourage officials to seek goal displacement and means substitution. The former strategy restates objectives, allowing resources to be shifted from programs exhibiting a decreasing rate of productivity to those where added resources are likely to increase the rate of productivity. The latter strategy promotes a search for alternative production techniques, including possible improvements in capital/labor ratios, an important efficacy determinant. Reflecting my experience, budget officers who use the lens of marginal productivity to look at different expenditure aggregations (using different production techniques and employing different resource mixes) will always find the exercise illuminating.

I. KEY IDEAS and CONDITIONING FACTORS

The use of benefit/cost calculations can also provide a platform for objective comparisons. However, the technique requires the monetary specification of benefits, selection of an interest rate and calculations about the value of benefits over time. Difficulties in monetizing estimated benefits limit its application, especially to public service programs.

Notwithstanding the difficulties of application, the two techniques are so valuable in providing insight and bases for objective judgment that budget officers are never wrong in organizing and presenting data arrays concerning marginal productivity and benefit/cost relationships. The very terms should frequently grace their vocabulary, reinforced in practice with skill and determination.

Do formats and procedures alter budget decisions? In the Preface to his influential book, *Government Budgeting,* 1956, Jesse Burkhead answered the question affirmatively by stating his conviction that the way in which revenue and expenditure are grouped for decision-making is the most important aspect of budgeting. Many other competent observers, including management guru, Peter Drucker, have dwelled on the decision-making importance of the organization of information. See "Technology, Management and Society," 1977, page 137, for his observation that the "organization of information is often more important to the ability to perceive and act than analysis and understanding of the information."

Over the decades, budget officers have taken a lively interest in this line of thought, and rightly so, given their abject dependence on information. Since the 1949 Hoover Commission recommended that the United States Government install "performance" budgeting, countless governments have experimented with results-oriented budget formats and procedures. These efforts certainly support Jesse Bulkhead's contention that the organization of information influences decisions. By trying to closely associate anticipated results with allocation decisions, these efforts also directed attention to a key problem of public budgeting: efficacious implementation.

Budgetary Thought for Budget Officers

If concerns about budget implementation are focused on expenditure events, the controls and accounting associated with the line-item form of budgeting certainly suffice. If, however, governments adopt some form of results-oriented budgeting, implementation concerns expand to embrace fulfillment of programmatic intentions. In pure line-item budgets, appropriation authorities fund the continued operation of administrative units. Beyond funding for agencies, the various alternatives to the line-item approach associate allocations with programmatic intentions variously specified as outputs, outcomes and impacts. This enrichment of the information base of the budgetary process provides conditions which enable appropriation authorities, should they be so inclined, to increase the proportion of allocations justified by formal (objective), rather than pragmatic (subjective) allocation criteria. This enrichment of the budgetary process also provides budget officers with manifold opportunities to promote the values of the effectiveness, efficiency and economy, the efficacy triad, in the provision of public services. It should be noted, in passing, that the formal decision criteria recommended by Exhibit 7.1, *Allocation Criteria*, include service standards expressing the public's interest in "equity calculations," as well as those applying the efficacy triad.

Further, the idea that the budget-related decisions of accountable officials should promote the values of efficacy and equity in government programs has significant institutional ramifications. After all, ideas (and policies and practices) depend on institutions for effect. If persistently pursued, official interests in efficacy and equity necessarily affect allocation policies, requiring results-oriented budget formulation, adoption, and implementation procedures. This, in turn affects budget office staffing and organization, accounting arrangements, and planning practices.

It is truly said that implementation is a serious weakness of public budgeting, its "Achilles' Heel," so to speak. The necessary "tools" of implementation are readily at hand, but not usually found "working hand-in-hand." As more expansively explored in Part Eight, the recommended

I. KEY IDEAS and CONDITIONING FACTORS

"tools" of implementation embrace inter-related administrative determinants, requiring firm institutionalization. These are 1) effective articulation and use of performance information; 2) an elaborate, flexible classification and coding scheme; 3) accounting procedures which facilitate the aggregation of non-monetary performance data, formally correlated with measures of effort and monetary data; and 4) continuous management utilization of four inter-related instruments of budget implementation. These four instruments are a) work plans, b) allotments, c) periodic formal performance reviews and d) timely corrective action.

Effective budgeting (attainment of performance objectives) is best assured by using an institutional framework integrating these determinants and instruments, with accounting procedures providing the glue. As stressed in Part Eight, these determinants are mutually reinforcing, the absence or limp implementation of one reduces the effectiveness of the others.

The commentaries that follow expand on the force and effect of these key ideas and conditioning factors. They also offer prescriptions for the application of preferred practices designed to incline the thinking of budget officers (and other concerned readers) along productive lines of inquiry and action. Each preferred practice has a natural foundation in public finance work and each may have an ideal development. Taken together, and applied, I believe that they provide the elements of a general model of exemplary practice. Also, taken together, they provide budget officers with a comprehensive evaluation framework. In cases where practice falls short of the suggested ideal, the model points the way to improvement.

This discussion of key ideas and conditioning factors closes with a rather pessimistic observation about the ever-evolving circumstances in which budget officers pursue their occupation. Since at least World War II, the budgetary environment of all levels of government in the United States has been increasingly affected by the willingness of legislative bodies to 1) "mandate" government subsidies based on "entitlement" 2) authorize categorical, formula-based subsidies, and 3) authorize conditional subsidies that have financial and programmatic "strings attached." This expansive reliance on legislatively-determined subsidies (by whatever name) reduces the budgetary discretion of both the benefactors and the beneficiaries. .(As a case in point, it takes a courageous local budget officer, indeed, to forward consequential reasons to decline a federal or state grant – after all, it's "free money!") In addition to introducing rigidities into the budget process by making the appropriations process, and thus, budget analysis and deliberation, less comprehensive and relevant, this subsidy-strewn environment effectively weakens accountability by separating revenue-raising from spending.

II. THE BUDGET OFFICER

In modern governments, budget officers work at the intersection of programmatic and financial values—a sort of "conflict central." Although countless other officials must take sides in the conflict between programmatic and financial values, none are so continuously occupied by the demand for critical judgment about the worth of things. The demand for their thinking is best understood by relating their role and persona to the requirements and tendencies of modern society. These requirements and tendencies were briefly noted in my introductory remarks.

Given the constant flow of disclosures, one gains an impression that a significant proportion of public expenditure is wasted by the misuse, underuse and abuse of assets; by duplication, system failure, and poor inter-agency coordination; not to mention, fraud and mal-adapted production techniques. Who, but budget officers are expected to stand as a bulwark against government ineffectiveness, inefficiency and profligacy?

The demand for the thinking of budget officers is also related to the occupational structure of contemporary governments. Obviously, governments pursue their policy and programmatic goals by employing persons with appropriate knowledge and skills. Typically, these employees identify their occupational specialties with that compelling abstraction, the "public interest." Physicians and epidemiologists press the primacy of their concerns for public health. Engineers stress the necessities of infrastructure. Teachers advance public education as the priority interest of society. This tendency of occupational specialists to identify their occupational interest with the public interest is an indispensable element in the determination of public policy. Their programmatic claims and proposed budget allocations provide gist for the mills of government. However, and very important, modern democratic governments have proven especially vulnerable to the pressure of special pleas. It is equally obvious that, at any given time, resource constraints limit the ability of any given government to fund and/or finance the manifold budget proposals advanced by specialists and special pleaders.

Clearly, a solvent treasury is also a public interest requiring respect, and an institutional buttress!

True, budget officers are also specialists — with this basic difference: Rather than pressing special pleas, they are recruited and retained to assess the relative merit of all proposed claims against the resources of their government's treasury. Wooed by many interested parties, budget officers have but one mistress: their government treasury.

With reference to their key task, their advice concerning the intrinsic and relative merit of proposed allocations should rest on criteria testing proposed programs and projects for effectiveness, efficiency and economy — the efficacy triad.

(An author's aside: Ideally, a criteria-based budget should result from such advice. Regrettably, given the politics of the budgetary process, budget officers can only dream about this ideal impact.)

Lest it be discounted as subjective and partisan, the counsel of budget officers must be grounded on transparent criteria, efficacy calculations and scholarship. Advice implies criteria, perceived as objective or subjective. As is widely acknowledged, budget allocations tend to be justified by subjective criteria. Accordingly, to counter this tendency, disinterested budget officers are challenged to expand the influence of objective tests of merit in the budget process. Part Seven, *Key Task: Assessing the Merit of Allocations*, describes ways and means of meeting this challenge.

II. THE BUDGET OFFICER

In addition to advice concerning the intrinsic and relative merit of proposed budget allocations, every well-ordered government expects reasoned advice from its budget officers on the factors conditioning budget size, scope and programmatic intentions, including, but not limited to, socio-economic considerations, resource availability and operational feasibility. Budget officers are expected to contribute to official thinking about such considerations. This requires that budget officers possess appropriate mental fitness. Obviously, the requisite knowledge, skill and mental disposition have implications for the academic preparation sought in recruits, and their subsequent education when on the job.

My thinking on the vital subject of budget officer education, immediately summarized below, is explored at length in my note concluding this book.

The required mental fitness rests on a tripod comprising 1) appropriate academic preparation, 2) lessons drawn from pertinent on-the-job experience, and 3) continuing education in useful subjects, tools and techniques.

1) **Academic Preparation**. If sufficiently emphasized, academic experience can inculcate habits of scholarship, promote logical thinking about complex problems, and develop competence in written and spoken expression of facts, interpretations and conclusions. Budget officers assess values reflectively by using techniques of scholarship, i.e., evidence and logic. The development of a scholarly disposition deserves emphasis because the work of budget officers requires the reflective treatment of values, as well as cold calculations. "Scholarship" produces systematic knowledge, that is, knowledge based on 1) an adequate, reliable assembly of information, (based on the crucial techniques of literature search and field inspection), 2) scrupulous regard for sources, 3) judicious

weighing of the evidence, and 4) conclusions drawn by means of clear, consistent, and cogent reasoning. These qualifications and dispositions are most comprehensively nurtured by a liberal arts curriculum, braced with courses in science and math, including statistics.

Because expenditure and revenue proposals are so often justified by reference to numerical arrays and relationships, budget officers need to master the techniques of statistical inference and mathematical modeling. Further, budget officers should adhere to standard criteria for systematic application of statistical tests and accepted standards.

This emphasis on general knowledge, critical thinking and facile expression is particularly relevant for budget officers serving governments of general jurisdiction, where diverse programs involve varied arts and sciences. Consequently, budget officers should be able to understand and assess the impact of art and science on the society their government serves. This proposition assumes familiarity with sociological conceptions as well. Said another way, budget officer academic preparation should produce keen observers of *la comedie humaine* (with credit due Horore Balzac for the phrase.)

2) **On-the-job Experience.** The importance of on-the-job experience in the development of effective budget officers cannot be overstated, nor should the impediments to development be underestimated. To attain the desired enhancements in competence, the work time of budget officers must be strictly programmed. (Daily administrative tasks which tie budget officers to their desks are

II. THE BUDGET OFFICER

the chief impediments to enhancing their knowledge and skill.) On principle, the work time of budget officers should be allocated three ways: 1/3 desk-time, including the tasks related to budget formulation and documentation; 1/3 programmatic interaction, including field trips, site visits and dynamic performance monitoring; and 1/3 decision-related programmatic research. Also, on principle, budget officers should be sequentially assigned to different programmatic sectors to broaden their subject-matter knowledge. This rotation also helps budget officers maintain a comprehensive view of multi-sector programs and their inter-relationships. To the same end, rotation arrangements may include brief deployments to work in program agencies. Usually, budget officers who regularly visit the work sites and staff of assigned program agencies are significantly affected by what they see and hear. Site visits permit them to become better acquainted with the scientific-technical basis of programmatic work, and its nomenclature. Equally important, site visits provide opportunities to observe and evaluate the conditions of work in programmatic agency environments.

To facilitate their research, budget officers are well advised to maintain program evaluation and development files related to their programmatic assignments. It is particularly important to prepare notes for future reference on issues, problems and opportunities surfacing during budget reviews, when the pressure of time does not permit in-depth reflection. Following budget adoption, these file notes serve to stir memories and stimulate imagination. Such files help to set relevant research agendas. Need I add that complaints and criticism are especially valuable additions to research-oriented program evaluation and development files.

3) **Continuing Education.** Over the course of their careers, budget officers should continue their education in useful subjects, tools and techniques. A variety of media are available to enhance subject-matter knowledge, foster the habits of scholarship and improve computational proficiency. (In this respect, the availability of "on-line, remote learning" has substantially removed the impediments of time, travel and expense to continuing education.) Further, this injunction is applicable to all officials working in any given jurisdiction. Program agencies usually employ numerous specialists who received their formal education years before, and who have failed to keep up with changes in their field. Budget officers can help to combat this serious problem by supporting arrangements for the continuing education of programmatic staffs. This endeavor should be an integral component of a budget policy to encourage and support programmatic and procedural innovation.

Moreover, every well-ordered government expects budget officers to effectively participate in budget procedures which 1) foster policy and managerial planning; 2) produce reliable expenditure estimates, balanced to prudent estimates of revenue; and 3) promote performance and timely goal attainment:

1) **Policy and Managerial Planning.** Part Six, *Preliminary Work*, provides an extensive commentary on the "front end" of the budget cycle. As recommended therein, the preliminary work phase concludes with the formulation of a "Revenue Mobilization Methodology" and a related

II. THE BUDGET OFFICER

"Fiscal and Budgetary Perspective." Ideally, these reports influence the content of the "Call for Estimates" initiating the budget formulation and documentation process. As emphasized in Part Six, the planning process and composition of the three documents requires the strong, unremitting participation of assigned budget officers.

2) **Reliable Estimates.** Since 1494, when the monk, Luca Pacioli, codified the rules of double entry bookkeeping, accountants have employed effective methods to control error in the recording and reporting of financial amounts. Although budgets rest on accounting foundations, the allocated amounts are estimates, seldom validated by experience as budgetary results rarely match estimates. In budgetary practice, a "good" estimate accurately forecasts the final amount, with a tolerable allowance for the inevitable variance. Consequently, a "good" budget minimizes the amount of variation between adopted estimates and the resulting revenue and expenditure.

Program officials are the main source of variance as they tend to systematically understate available inventories, overstate rates of expenditure and inflate expenditure estimates as a defense against allocation reductions expected during the budget review process. Given the upward bias of estimates in allocation proposals, budget officers must examine the basis for all estimates, seeking to enhance the accuracy of estimates, that is, estimates that minimize the amount of variance that will eventually develop during budget implementation. Obviously, this is an undesirable situation as this requirement drains away precious time from the important task of determining the merit of proposed allocations. More observations on the estimating process are included in Part Three, *The Grammar of Budgeting.*

To be sure, budget officers must strive to reduce their own contributions to the amount of estimating variance. They often contribute to variances by recommending arbitrary adjustments in allocation proposals without effecting corresponding adjustments in operating conditions. Budget officers can reduce their contributions to error by using techniques of data control during data transfers, aggregation processes, research projects, and report preparation and presentation. These techniques include such practices as "proving" calculations, cross-footing, "spread-sheet" displays, plus and minus controls, batching to isolate error, proof-reading, making changes at the lowest level of aggregation, following strict rules for rounding, etc.

3) **Performance and Timely Goal Attainment.** The role of budget officers in the goal attainment process is expansively explored in Part Eight, *Implementation Methodology: Dynamic Monitoring.* As described in Part Eight, effective implementation requires a quartet of inter-related administrative instruments, 1) work plans, 2) allotments, 3) performance reviews, and 4) corrective action. As stressed in Part Eight, unless budget officers actively support the entire process, budget implementation procedures will be fragmented, weak, even non-existent. Undoubtedly, without budget officer support and monitoring, allotment processes degenerate into meaningless accounting rituals, providing program leaders with little incentive to plan and perform. This is important because a ritualistic or non-existent allotment

II. THE BUDGET OFFICER

process usually correlates with a weak or non-existent performance review system. Similarly, as pointed out in Part Eight, an effective, dynamic performance review system depends on active budget officer involvement for its effectiveness.

At this point, consult Exhibit 2.1, *A Model Budget Officer Job Description*. Presented as a general model, it lists activities and/or tasks required of a typical budget officer serving in a typical government of general jurisdiction. As a general model, it rests on a number of assumed conditions which may not be present in particular circumstances:

First, it assumes that the jurisdiction employs an "executive budget," that is, the jurisdiction's chief executive integrates the disparate budgets of program agencies in a single document submitted for review and adoption by an appropriation authority. Second, administrative budget officers work in a program agency or a central budget unit, variously called a department, division, or office. With the exception of Tasks 1 and 4, the model job description does not apply to budget officers serving appropriation authorities. Third, the assumed jurisdiction has a budget planning process, culminating in the issuance of a call for estimates to formulate a budget for the upcoming period.

Exhibit 2.1 A Model Budget Officer Job Description

ACTIVITY/TASK	PARTICULARS
Formulate periodic personal work plans.	List of activities/tasks, work hours, performance indicators, and milestones. If in a budget unit, personal work plans must be coordinated with the plans of other budget officers.
Participate in the preliminary work of budgeting	Execute tasks related to the organization and management of the budget anticipatory process. With special reference to Fiscal and Budgetary Perspective, assist responsible program leaders, knowledgeable individuals and interested parties to draft well-documented papers on significant issues, problems and opportunities facing the jurisdiction.
Facilitate budget formulation	Assist program agency staff to comply with documentation requirements in formulation of budget proposals, especially those officials new to the task.
Assess the intrinsic and relative merit of budget proposals, submitting recommendations.	Applying analytical skill, examine proposed allocations, critically evaluate the supporting evidence, exercise judgment on the merits of proposals, recommend revisions where indicated. Given time limits, proficiency in executing this task depends on the quality of previous research and familiarity with programmatic sites, activities and staff.
Participate in the composition of the jurisdiction's proposed budget.	Assist in producing "finished copy" of the proposed budget to be recommended for adoption by the jurisdiction's appropriation authority. As a cohesive, coherent assembly of data arrays and interpretive text, the submitted budget may be transmitted in book and/or electronic form.
Provide information to appropriation authorities during budget adoption proceedings.	As requested, respond to inquiries from legislators, assist program leaders in legislative hearings and workshops, assist the chief executive in budget justifications and, if needed, assist in the composition of veto messages.
Monitor budget implementation.	Support the conduct of periodic formal performance reviews. Assist in executing corrective action in cases of impending failure to attain goals. Provide advice and assistance on the allotment of appropriations, transfers and supplemental appropriations. Assist accountable program leaders in the preparation of expenditure and revenue estimates required for treasury cash flow projections.
Conduct research.	Pursue an agenda of research and reflection on the ends and means of assigned programs.
Conduct field visitations.	Visit program staff at work sites, encouraging innovative solutions to budgetary and performance problems.
Provide training.	Conduct formal and "ad hoc" training in performance improvement and budget formulation and documentation.

Finally, the assumed jurisdiction employs a formal, periodic performance review process, supported by budget officers. Work plan formulation, the first activity/task listed in the job description, is not only intrinsically important (as good practice), but is important in terms of the leadership concepts of precept and example. As emphasized above

II. THE BUDGET OFFICER

in my comments concerning performance and timely goal attainment, budget officers are expected to be key participants in budget implementation, thus, they must practice what is preached.

In addition to required knowledge and skill, the model job description assumes that effective budget officers are distinguished by their orientation, that is, well-developed mental habits that enable them to filter the facts and values assailing their senses to concentrate their thought and effort on truly important ways to evaluate the worth of budget allocations. *Budget officers must train their minds to think in terms of the subject.* As physicists think in terms of masses, forces and vectors, budget officers should first examine a proposed allocation in terms of problematic causes, programmatic intentions and performance conditions. To facilitate this examination, budget officers require proposal documentation that:

a) Defines program rationale: the issues/problems/opportunities to be addressed.
b) States goal(s) in a multi-year perspective.
c) Identifies collaborators and affected parties.
d) Identifies conditions required for goal attainment.
e) Formulates the preferred solution(s) and a work plan(s).
f) Formulates a budget in a multi-year perspective.
g) Identifies alternatives considered, but rejected, and why.

Guidelines concerning budget formulation and documentation are discussed in detail in Part Five, *Formulation and Documentation Guidelines*. If documented as recommended, this programmatic information should permit budget officers to assess the *intrinsic* merit of a proposed allocation. The thought process is capsulated by the equation, $y = f(x)$, which describes the production function of public budgets. In this equation, "x" equals the allocated resources, "y" equals output/

outcome/impact, monetized if possible, if not, then specified in numerical terms. The "f" symbolically denotes the production technique, such as, police patrols, inspection, teaching, etc. The application of this formula is explored in Part Seven, *Key Task: Assessing the Merit of Allocations.*

Once satisfied concerning the intrinsic merit of a proposed allocation, budget officers must next assess its *relative* merit. What share of available resources, if any, does it deserve? This is the fundamental, and most perplexing, question of budgeting! Responding to that question is easier if budget officers have thought deeply about how to modify the existing allocation pattern and production techniques, that is, identify opportunities for goal displacement and means substitution. Experience indicates that, year-after-year, budgets tend to perpetuate programmatic patterns, changing slightly in total, and even less in shares. Programs and their budgets gather inertia. Usually, program proponents classify their proposals as "inescapable recurrent" expenditure even though, in many cases, program rationale may be weak, or weakening as times change. Redirecting allocations from ineffective and/or inefficient programs to new initiatives enables officials to address new problems without additional taxes or loans. By concentrating on relationships between applied resources and results, $y = f(x)$, budget officials can provide recommendations which can help rationalize the allocation pattern.

II. THE BUDGET OFFICER

Exhibit 2.2 A Model Work Program

> Invest approximately 1/3 of annual work hours in research and reflection on the ends and means of assigned programs, including active participation in the composition of multi- year Fiscal and Budgetary Perspectives initiating the annual budget cycle.
>
> Invest approximately 1/3rd of annual work hours in field work with program personnel, including active participation in the management and conduct of periodic performance reviews. This plan of consultation and training should embrace 1) field trips, systematically visiting program staff and their work sites, encouraging innovative solutions to budgetary and performance problems, and 2) the conduct of formal and "ad hoc" training in performance improvement techniques and budget formulation, documentation requirements, problem definition, goal statements, etc
>
> Reserve approximately 1/3 of annual work hours for desk-time, including the tasks related to budget formulation.
>
> Apply well-understood criteria to govern the handling and interpretation of programmatic data, including the application of statistical tests and generally accepted standards of logic and inference.
>
> Seek and maintain a reputation for producing assigned work outputs on time, providing program personnel with precept and example.
>
> Concentrate on the relationship of input to results, avoiding arbitrary allotment adjustments without collateral adjustment in associated performance indicators.
>
> Concentrate on the relationship of organization units to one another, recognizing that budget officers have unique responsibilities for the proper ordering of unit-to-unit linkages throughout the entire government. (All too frequently, the sources of inefficacious administration can be traced to maladaptive relationships between centralized special process units, such as, planning, human resources, purchasing, legal, information technology engineering, property and vehicle maintenance, etc., and the program agencies they serve.)

Budget officers must look to the future, viewing past and present experience as *experiments* requiring evaluation and interpretation, rather than as determinants. The inertial factor noted above, and the ever-present proclivity of policy officials to put off decisions adversely affecting interests they favor, justify a premium on efforts to foresee and shape the future. In concert with planners (if employed by the jurisdiction), budget officers must cultivate habits of mind, expression and action that draw possible future happenings (desired and undesired) into the conscious present at every opportunity. The budget officer's research agenda is the chief instrument fostering the cultivation of a future orientation. The strong participation of budget officers in the preliminary work of budgeting (see Part Six) also provides an opportunity to hone the indispensable habits of mind, expression and action that cultivate powers of foresight.

As prescribed in Exhibit 2.2, A *Model Work Program*, budget officers are advised to spend about one-third of their time in the field with program staff, one-third in research and reflection on the ends and means of assigned programs, and one-third on production tasks, such as the composition of the annual budget. The competency of budget officers accrues in direct proportion to the time devoted to field visitations and research. Budget offices need not be very large, but must have a talented staff, strongly supported by access to library resources, computer technology and the means to undertake systematic field investigations.

In terms of their job philosophy, certain lines of thinking and action should always distinguish budget officers, even when circumstances limit chances for application:

> First, it is the beginning of budgetary wisdom to assume that current allocations are to be treated as *experiments in programmatic action*, that is, variables requiring continuing proof of their efficacy, rather than as determinants of future appropriations. This philosophical orientation has significant consequences, especially with regard to a budget officer's research approach. (See the fourth point below)

II. THE BUDGET OFFICER

Second, relentlessly work to expand the proportion of allocations justified by formal, rather than pragmatic allocation criteria.

Third, never cease seeking to redirect allocations from ineffective and/or inefficient programs to new initiatives. Year-to-year, budgets tend to perpetuate programmatic patterns, changing slightly in total, and even less in shares. As noted above, and repeated here for emphasis, programs have inertia. Program proponents tend to classify their requests as "inescapable recurrent" expenditure even though, in many cases, program rationale may be weak, or weakening as times change. Redirecting allocations from ineffective and/or inefficient programs to new initiatives permits officials to address new problems within a pattern of stable revenues. Attaining this desired rationalization of allocation patterns requires budget officers to concentrate their attention on relationships between input and performance indicators.

Forth, apply the principles of "action research," rather than a "study-and-report" mode of analysis. As suggested by Kurt Lewin, action research involves an iterative series of steps involving planning, action and evaluation, then re-planning, etc., all conducted by a researcher in concert with those subject to the outcome of the research. In contrast, the study-and-report mode of analysis is conducted solely by researchers following a well-known sequence of steps: a) problem definition, b) hypothesis formulation, c) assembly of pertinent evidence, d) weighing evidence, and e) proposing and reporting recommended solutions. However, as is also well known, in political and bureaucratic environments, study-and-report research results have a low probability of acceptance and implementation. All too frequently, such reports are put on a shelf and there gather dust. To avoid this fate, research undertaken by budget officers must be decision-related, not undertaken as an academic search for knowledge for its own sake. The interactive, iterative action research approach mitigates the risk of rejection by affected parties. Obviously an action research approach to programmatic problems enriches the field work of budget officers, giving it a practical focus. If done in good faith, budget officers are likely to find that program officials will be enthusiastic participants.

Fifth, subscribe to a philosophy of public finance and budgeting, even if the circumstances of their employment may limit application of its tenets. In terms of on-the-job effectiveness, it is important that budget officers should be known as persons of knowledge about public finance, and convictions about its proper practice. Distilled from my own experience and world view, I suggest that public officials in general, and budget officers in particular, subscribe to the following policies and procedures:

- Match desired services to financial resources, borrowing only for capital investments.

- Fund or finance only those services and projects which cannot be provided privately.

II. THE BUDGET OFFICER

- Require beneficiary payment for services, when technically possible.

- Minimize subventions. (Self-sufficiency at all levels of government.)

- Strive for programmatic effectiveness, efficiency and economy (the efficacy triad) by employing:

    1) Solution-centered, Results-oriented Budgets (Cost Center Formats)
    2) Work Plans
    3) Allotments
    4) Dynamic Monitoring (Periodic Formal Performance Reviews)
    5) Corrective Action

Sixth, promote the following practices related to a jurisdiction's balance sheet:

- Maintenance of a minimum end-of-period cash balance.

- Periodic composition and publication of "pro-forma" statements estimating the impact of budget implementation on the government's financial position at the year's end.

- Depreciation reserves for orderly replacement of facilities and the timely acquisition of state-of-the-art technology.

- An annual program of investments in public facilities which equals or exceeds asset depreciation.

- An annual program of investment focused on attaining and maintaining efficient, effective capital/labor ratios.

Before proceeding, the injunction concerning the efficacy triad deserves further comment. Succeeding with dynamic monitoring requires the active engagement of budget officers, who must encourage the composition of work plans at every supervisory level. Otherwise, periodic performance reviews and subsequent authorization of allotments will lack solid reference. Without information gleaned from participating in a systematic performance review system, budget officers will have difficulty in correlating allotments with work plans, supporting corrective action fostering goal attainment, and providing cash managers with accurate information on expenditure plans. The vital subject of budget implementation is explored in detail in Part Eight, *Implementtation Methodology: Dynamic Monitoring.*

Turning to the ethical dimensions of the job, it is a commonplace understanding that public officials tend to take the trappings of their office very seriously. Apparently, one's office easily becomes the measure of all things. Indulging their conceit, and masking their fear, they strive to defend and extend the power of their office, perhaps to the detriment of programmatic purposes.

Budget officers also share this human propensity, but must suppress its expression. They must possess enough self-awareness to curb its expression in themselves as well as possess enough acuity and courage to recognize and help curb its deleterious influence on policies, projects and programs put forward for public funding and/or finance. Budget officers possessing this essential mental quality help their governments to reduce the application of subjective criteria in the budget formulation process.

II. THE BUDGET OFFICER

Continuing on this ethical plane, to practice their craft efficaciously, budget officers must maintain good relationships with key officials, especially program leaders. All too frequently this relationship is defined in terms of "control", rather than "analysis" and "service." "No" should not be the characteristic response. Moreover, too many budget officers devote a disproportionate amount of time to expenditure analysis, slighting program assessment and other critical dimensions of policy and managerial practice. Given that program officials will likely see a strong focus on expenditure as disinterest in their work, a budget officer never goes wrong in showing keen interest in production. Indeed, budget officers should so conduct themselves that program officials perceive them as more interested in goal attainment than costs.

Specifically, this means that budget officers should seek and maintain a deserved reputation for 1) seeking to understand program problems, 2) defining performance in relative terms, trends and tendencies, rather than absolutes, and 3) using measurements to spur performance improvement, not for fault-finding and fixing blame. By virtue of their ability to study and reflect, budget officers are frequently in a position to encourage program leaders to innovate, and should do so. Further, in conducting implementation-related research and field work, budget officers should participate vigorously in performance reviews and, in particular, actively support program officials in their goal attainment efforts. Finally, budget officers must seek and maintain a reputation for personal efficacy, providing an example to all.

Relationships between budget officers and program officials can become tense, and ethically charged at that point in the budget formulation process when budget officers must express assessments about the intrinsic or relative merit of proposed allocations. If interactions and communications have been constructive, as outlined above, these assessments should not surprise accountable program officials. More often than not, budget officers will be recommending allocation modifications, in effect substituting their judgment for that of program officials.

Budgetary Thought for Budget Officers

In this conflict, no ethical issue arises if budget officers avoid the appearance and reality of arbitrary action.

Recommendations about proposed allocations should be conveyed forthwith to accountable program officials, citing reasons related to the efficacy triad and other allocation criteria, giving them an opportunity to respond. Further, in well-ordered jurisdictions, program officials will be afforded an avenue of appeal prior to final decisions on allocations to be submitted to the appropriation authority.

III. THE GRAMMAR OF BUDGETING

Typically, the public budgeting process has a number of defined elements and an order of usage — a grammar of sorts. Rather like watchful and active grammarians, budget officers, and their accounting colleagues, work to maintain the integrity of the process. The key elements are 1) the instruments of the right to spend, embracing appropriations, allocations and allotments, and 2) a chart of accounts, listing revenue and expenditure classifications and codes. The employment of these elements is bounded and directed by a time-specific budget cycle. System maintenance is a necessary preoccupation of budget officers. In this Part, we explore their role as "grammarians," accompanied by comments on the work of accountants, as indispensable allies. The budget officer's critical role in budget implementation is considered at length in Part Eight,

The Right to Spend

Government budgeting is legally tied to the concept of appropriation. Budgets are adopted when proper authorities vote to accept expenditure estimates, thereby converting them into appropriations. According to Webster's Dictionary, to appropriate *"is to set aside for a specific use."* Appropriations establish the right to spend public funds for public purposes, and the limits of such spending. In democratic governments, the power to authorize spending public funds is assigned to lawmaking bodies. The Constitution of the United States provides a very clear statement to that effect:

> *No money shall be drawn from the treasury, but in consequence of appropriations made by law..."*

Similar provisions may be found in the organic law of all democratically organized governments.

The appropriation power is usually restricted by a variety of laws and regulations which define and limit this authority. For an appropriation to be valid, all legal prerequisites, or conditions precedent, must be observed. While the exact mix varies, the laws and regulations governing the budget process usually include provisions similar to those listed below:

- The illegality of expenditure made without appropriation.

- Appropriation for public purposes only.

- A calendar of budgetary events.

- Budget and appropriation formats.

- The identity and duty of officials who have budgetary roles.

- Appropriations justified by estimates by competent authorities.

- Consideration of all budget proposals within a specified time.

- Appropriations "balanced" by estimated available revenues.

III. THE GRAMMAR OF BUDGETING

- Borrowing limited to asset acquisitions.

- Public hearing and referenda requirements.

- Mandatory appropriations for debt service and pensions.

- Accounting, auditing and reporting of budgetary activity.

The concept, "allocation," is both a generic term referring to any budgeted amount and a term describing the division and distribution of an appropriation to support programmatic activities identified by concept and code in a jurisdiction's chart of accounts.

An allotment refers to a distribution of an allocation by a specified time period. Budget officers are deeply involved in the allocation and allotment of appropriations, especially the latter, as allotments are one of the four principal instruments of budget implementation. The role of allotments, employed in concert with three other instruments comprising an "implementation quartet." is explored in Part Eight, *Implementation Methodology*: *Dynamic Implementation,*

In addition to granting limited spending rights to public agency officials, legislatures may use the appropriation power to review the general thrust of governmental activity and, in many cases, the specific conduct of administrative work. Elected legislatures try to use the "power of the purse" to maintain control of programs and procedures of administrative agencies. Justified as "oversight," this power is a potent addition to their general legislative authority. Oversight is usually exercised by subject matter legislative committees during the fiscal period. Committee hearings and workshops may take testimony from accountable program officials and interested parties. These oversight sessions are usually regarded as serious events, requiring the time and attention of relevant budget officers.

Budget officers are acutely conscious of the passage of time, marked by the beginning and end of a jurisdiction's fiscal period — typically one year. The essential continuity of the budgeting process, as well as its repetitive nature, is captured by the term, the "budget cycle."

Budget Cycle

The formulation and adoption of next year's budget occurs during the latter part of the current year's budget. Exhibit 6.1, *Budget Cycle Components*, displayed in Part Six, *Preliminary Work*, places recommended practices within the major phases of an idealized annual budget cycle. As shown in Exhibit 6.1, the anticipatory phase should feature the development of a fiscal and budgetary perspective, including 1) an assessment of issues, problems and opportunities facing the jurisdiction, 2) a revenue mobilization methodology and 3) identification of priority proposals recommended for action in the upcoming budget. See Part Six for details. Also note that the fiscal year has been divided into quarters establishing periodic checkpoints for the exercise of formal, periodic performance reviews. As dynamic, rather than static events, these performance reviews should be conducted two-thirds through each quarter, providing a month for corrective action in those cases where the review indicates probable failure to attain projected goals by the quarter's end. This emphasis on dynamic monitoring rests on the belief that performance reporting after the reporting period is over is an ineffective ritual, serving an archival rather than management function. See Part Eight for details.

The Metaphysics of Budgeting: Classification

Formats are important! Even though the influence of form on thought can be overstated, people do tend to think about what comes before them. Budgetary classifications thus shape budgetary discourse, channeling the thought of participants in the budgetary process, defining the terms of debate, discussions and, most important, deeds.

Although a jurisdiction's accountants are the custodians of its chart of accounts, which prescribes labels and codes for budget-related financial transactions, the classification scheme, itself, is also a prime

III. THE GRAMMAR OF BUDGETING

concern of budget officers and, most critically, the subject program managers. Therefore, consultation among affected parties should precede the designation of identifiers.

As noted in Exhibit 3.1, *Budget Classification Concepts,* a chart of accounts can embrace numerous classification concepts. In a shorthand way, expressive classification titles (and associated codes) assigned to budgetary transactions help define the "who, what, where, when, how and why" of revenues and expenditures. By providing clues to budgetary purposes.the budgetary chart of accounts serves a metaphysical function.

Exhibit 3.1 Budget Classification Concepts

Organization	Accounting	Configuration	Policy	Performance
Ministry	Fund	Class	Goal	Function
Agency	Account	Category	Objective	Cost Center
Department	Object	Component	Service	Responsibility Center
Division	Item	Element	Program	Activity
Bureau	Source	Time	Project	Task
Section	Fixed	Space (Area)		Job
Unit	Variable			

The advent of various forms of results-oriented budgeting focused academic and political attention on classification schemes. In seeking to relate allocations to intentions and expected results, results-oriented budgeting requires that expenditures be aggregated, or summarized, by expressive titles. Exhibit 3.1 identifies 31 bases for the aggregation of costs, grouped in five classification "families," testifying to the diversity of classification concepts found in various budget documents. Typically, jurisdictions mix their identifiers, drawing terms from more than one classification family. With reference to performance budgets, knitting these aggregations together requires an elaborate hierarchy of summaries. In the following illustration, accounting, organizational, and programmatic identifiers are arranged in typical hierarchical order.

Budgetary Thought for Budget Officers

    Fund
        Function
            1st Level of Organization
                2nd Level of Organization
                    3rd Level of Organization
                        Activity/Task (Cost center at lowest supervisory level)
                            Type of Cost
                                Item of Expenditure or Revenue

    Above the base level, each classification summarizes costs identified with the classification below it. This hierarchical approach provides a basis for supervisory accountability at every organizational level, and provides a basis for efficacy evaluations.

    As used here, the term, "cost center" applies to any aggregation of costs (defined as disbursements, expenditure or expense) which can be associated with 1) a manager and 2) an indicator(s) of results. Like bricks in a wall, cost centers provide basic units of budget construction. Once the accountable officials have estimated costs for proposed activities/tasks conducted by "front-line" unit supervisors, these unit-by-unit cost center estimates are aggregated according to hierarchical responsibility until a total budget results. Looking upward from the basic cost centers, results-oriented budgets comprise an ascending order of increasingly *inclusive* cost centers, until a cost center representing the total budget is reached. This summary total, and its array of subsidiary aggregations, must be identified with an accounting entity, usually defined as a "Fund," In common usage, budgets supporting programmatic activities are assigned to "general" or "consolidated" funds. Appropriations for "projects" (additions to fixed assets) are usually assigned to "capital" funds. An array of "cost center classifications," and the associated funding and financing sources, provides a designated fund with a "chart of accounts" for recording and controlling transactions. Looking downward, a total budget is "disaggregated", "decomposed," or "broken down" into a descending order of increasingly exclusive cost centers until the unique base aggregations is reached.

III. THE GRAMMAR OF BUDGETING

Exhibit 3.2 Sample Classification and Code Scheme

Expenditure Ledger

1	2	3	4	5	6	7	8	

01 General
    2 Public Safety
        3 Fire Protection Department
            2 Fire Prevention Division
                2 License and Permit Section
                    3 Inspection
                        01 Type of Cost: Variable
                            101 Salaries

Revenue Ledger

01 General
    2 Public Safety
        3 Fire Protection Department
            2 Fire Prevention Division
                2 License and Permit Section
                    3 Inspection
                        05 Regulatory Revenues
                            006 Sprinkler Permits

Performance Ledger

01 General
    2 Public Safety
        3 Fire Protection Department
            2 Fire Prevention Division
                2 License and Permit Section
                    3 Inspection
                        02 Sprinkler System Tests
                            002 Defects Corrected

Budgetary Thought for Budget Officers

The sample classification and code scheme displayed by Exhibit 3.2 uses the same set of classifications and codes for all code groups, except code groups 7 an 8. Using the same set of classifications and codes for the classification, recording and reporting of expenditure, revenue and performance data facilitates the coordination of program data for analysis and presentation. In addition, such a consolidated cost center record system could log and report types of effort, such as, workloads, work targets, staff paid hours, staff work hours, kilowatt hours and performance data drawn from reports and invoices submitted by contractors, etc. Moreover, assigning the same identifiers to program expenditures and program related revenues focuses managerial attention on net financial results (plus or minus) of program activity. As managers are customarily preoccupied with spending, a consolidated report showing net financial results acquaints them with revenue-raising necessities, encouraging them to recommend ways to increase program-related revenues.

Given the probability that jurisdictions using the fund concept to organize their accounting system will have more than nine funds, the sample classification and coding array shown in Exhibit 3.2 provides **Code Level 1** with two digits (1 to 99 possibilities), providing for the identification of 99 separate funds. As an example, Fund 1 is usually designated as a general, or consolidated fund, recording transactions related to a jurisdiction's array of service programs. Transactions related to capital projects are usually lodged together in a Fund designated for that purpose. Of course, if a jurisdiction has more than 99 funds, three or more digits will be required, depending on the number of funds. This qualification applies to all the codes listed in the sample classification and code scheme shown in Exhibit 3.2. In general, a proper philosophy of coding stresses economy in their use, specifying that no more digits will be provided than are needed, reducing coding effort and the possibility of coding error.

Code Level 2: One digit provides for the identification of 9 functions, such as general government, public safety, etc. **Code Level 3**: One digit (1 to 9) provides for the identification of 9 programs, departments,

III. THE GRAMMAR OF BUDGETING

services, etc. **Code Level 4**: One digit (1 to 9 possibilities) provides for the identification of 9 programs, subprograms, divisions, services, activities, etc. **Code Level 5**: One digit (1 to 9 possibilities) provides for the identification of 9 cost centers, such as, section, bureau, area, shift, crew, unit, squad, district, structure, etc. **Code Level 6**: One digit (1 to 9 possibilities –more may be required) provides for the identification of performance cost centers for specific jobs, tasks, projects, etc. **Code Level 7**: Two digits (1 to 99 possibilities), although only two numbers would be needed to record fixed and variable costs, codes 1 (variable) and 2 (fixed) respectively. Two digits are probably sufficient to identify regulatory revenues in most jurisdictions Code **Level 8**: Three digits (1 to 999 possibilities) for the identification of 999 commodity or item payments, such as salaries, gasoline, equipment repair, etc. The first digit can be used to designate major object classifications, such as 1, personal services, 2, non-personal expense, etc.

Exhibit 3.3 Purposes Validating Cost Centers

PURPOSE	COMMENT
Identify costs and work time for performance ratio calculations.	Such calculations justify cost center establishment.
Identify costs for review of resource mix options and/or alternative production techniques.	Requires jurisdiction's commitment to such examinations and resulting changes.
Identify costs to facilitate program research.	Requires jurisdiction's commitment to research agendas and consideration of research results.
Identify costs for pricing service charges.	Requires jurisdiction's commitment to such usage to justify cost center establishment.
Draw attention to outstanding problems and/or issues.	Costs can be reassigned to issue-oriented cost centers. Conversely, in stable, efficient programs, cost centers can be amalgamated by mergers and reassignments.
Identify costs for aggregation and comparison with costs of similar functions in other cost centers.	Requires evidence of jurisdiction's decision-related usage of such aggregations and comparisons to validate the establishment of cost centers.
Identify resource commitments for the implementation of salient policies.	Requires review of cost center arrays for excessive decomposition, as they may include more centers and levels than needed to confirm commitments.
Isolate costs which cannot be easily or accurately assigned to other cost centers.	Identifies "indirect," "fixed" or "common" costs of supervision, central process units, "overhead" items, etc. Two or more subsidiary cost centers within a cost center probably require a third, "residual," cost center to isolate the common costs of supporting services and/or resources.

Because they record coded classification schemes and the associated figures, ledgers recording the usage of resources are an important resource for program managers and budget officers, especially if they are working with results-oriented budgets. With reference to the use of expenditure ledgers, the location of controls on the incurrence of encumbrances and disbursements proved to be an important, and contentious, issue. In each jurisdiction, e resolution of this issue determines the fundamental design of its expenditure ledger. If the control points are associated with results-oriented "lump-sum" summaries (program, project, activity or task), rather than with expenditure summaries or objects of expenditure (salaries, supplies, etc.), these latter entries will be identified as analytical rather than control identifiers and codes, providing information only. In those governments where the leading accounting officials are unwilling to establish controls at a programmatic level (lump-sum), the managerial assumptions of results-oriented budgeting are seriously compromised. As cost centers are the fundamental building blocks of an accounting system supporting results-oriented budgeting, their establishment and adjustment to changed program conditions merits serious consideration by managers and the accounting staff.

Exhibit 3.4 presents a list of performance conceptions to be consulted when adding a cost center to the Chart of Accounts. An array of cost centers can be used dynamically for any of the purposes listed in Exhibit 3.3. For example, if a specific activity needs management attention, a cost center embracing its elements can be identified and established for research purposes. The research completed, the elements of the cost center in question can be merged into an associated cost center. Organizational and policy changes usually require changes in relevant cost center arrays. The application of the standards of the efficacy triad (effectiveness, efficiency, economy) test the managerial competence of public officials, and provide budget officers with criteria for their assessment of the intrinsic merit of proposed allocations.

III. THE GRAMMAR OF BUDGETING

Exhibit 3.4 Performance Conceptions

OUTPUT	Production quantities, measured in units of service or goods. As output can be increased at the expense of quality, volume measurements must be qualified by quality specifications (waiting time, accounting error rates, in-hospital infection rates, etc.).
OUTCOME or IMPACT	Consequences of output quantity, quality and distribution on society. Even when measurable, interpretation requires subjective evaluation.
EFFECTIVENESS	The degree of attainment of an ideal, a goal or an intention, calculated as a percentage with results serving as the numerator and the ideal, goal or intention numerically stated as the denominator. Interpretation requires comparative reference.
EFFICIENCY	The relationship (ratio) between a result and the resources (input) used to produce it, calculated by dividing results by input or the reverse. Interpretation requires comparative reference.
ECONOMY	Results obtained with minimum use of resources. An important management consideration, forestalling extravagant, wasteful expenditure –an ever-present possibility in public programs.

In addition to permitting an elaborate and flexible format, expenditure ledgers should be designed to assist program managers with the implementation of their budgets. This includes the following facilities:

- Recording and timely reporting of work hours charged to activities/tasks listed in Work Plans. (Because Work Plans are fundamentally based on work time calculations, this facility is as valuable to program managers as variable cost reporting.)

- Recording and timely reporting of the variable costs of activities/tasks listed in those Work Plans which are subordinate to controlling cost center allocations.

- Permitting program managers to enter budget reservations into the accounting system as contingent liabilities, especially requisitions for goods and services which have not yet reached the status of encumbrances, that is, contracts and purchase orders. (Because it tracks the status of obligations from source to settlement, this arrangement is especially useful in jurisdictions with centralized purchasing units with their inevitable service queues. The ability to reserve portions of available budget balances also facilitates the planning of operations.)

With regard to the input side of results-oriented budgets, government accountants tend to agree that management accounting systems would provide the best accounting support. However, in contrast to profit-oriented enterprises, governments lack compelling incentives to invest in this expensive elaboration of their accounting systems, especially for the service programs funded by general revenues. Similarly, when cost estimates, especially statements of total, or "full" cost are required to make important decisions, cost finding procedures can yield acceptable results. As research and analysis, rather than accounting, cost finding requires the assembly, evaluation and adjustment of relevant information drawn from various sources, including data provided by the formal accounting system, to derive the desired costs.

III. THE GRAMMAR OF BUDGETING

Because the chart of accounts determines the budget format, a vital matter, the adopted classification scheme should be subject to serious consideration and referenced to acknowledged criteria. (Obviously, such acknowledgement assumes happy collaboration between the jurisdiction's accountants, budget officers and the concerned program managers.) As noted by Exhibit 3.5, *Cost Center Criteria,* five concepts are advanced to test the validity of cost centers. The weight given to each criterion is an open question to be decided by the parties involved.

EXHIBIT 3.5 Cost Center Criteria

CRITERION	TEST
SIGNIFICANCE	Center aggregates costs devoted to an important purpose.
PRODUCTIVITY	Center linked to specific, measurable performance results.
ACCOUNTABILITY	Center assigned to a manager accountable for resource applications and performance.
REPORTABILITY	Center supported by procedures for recording, relating and reporting financial and performance data.
ACCEPTANCE	Center understood and endorsed by affected staff and interested parties.

Before continuing with a discussion of cost center criteria, we must note that the definition of "cost" is dependent on the accounting convention applied:

- If a budget is supported by cash accounting conventions, a cost center is a denoted aggregation of disbursements.

- If a budget is supported by "modified accrual" accounting conventions, treating "commitments" as disbursements, a cost center is a denoted aggregation of expenditure.

- If a budget is supported by accrual accounting conventions, a cost center is a denoted aggregation of expense.

Obviously, "costs," are the prime subject of budgetary thought and practice. However, as indicated above, amounts cited as "costs" may be computed and displayed in various ways, reflecting different conceptions of economics and accounting:

Most familiarly, cost estimates are formulated on a *cash* basis, that is, estimates are based on expected *disbursements*. Budget control is tighter if estimates are based on *expenditure*, a concept of cost which adds outstanding *encumbrances* (purchase orders), and, perhaps, *reservations*, to disbursements. At the highest level of accounting practice, costs may be calculated as *expenses*, a concept which aggregates cash, accruals and non-cash charges. Further, budgets are frequently organized to separate *direct* from *indirect* cost classifications, which results in understated service costs. Finally, costs may be defined and displayed as *total, fixed, variable, controllable, standard, unit, sunk* or *marginal*.

To be accurate and useful, costs and work time should be recorded promptly, as incurred. 'Direct" costs include salary payments for work time applied to specific activities/tasks. Operating costs clearly associated with specific activities also qualify as "direct" costs. "Indirect" costs include expenditures which benefit several activities, but can only be apportioned to these activities by formula. Examples include general supervisors and centralized process units. Allocation concepts include proportioning indirect costs by (a) direct cost proportions, salaries, for example, (b) direct work time distributions, and, best of all, (c) tracing work load distributions. General space-related expenses, such as,

III. THE GRAMMAR OF BUDGETING

electricity, rent, custodial services and maintenance, can be fairly allocated by the proportioning of total floor area used by specific activities. Vehicle expenses can be allocated by proportions of total mileage logged by staff assigned to specific activities.

In the final analysis, every indirect cost allocation formula is more or less arbitrary. Consequently, responsible officials should strive to find bases for allocation which are regarded as fair by those subject to it. Once settled on a fair formula, to protect the validity of comparisons, it should be consistently applied from period to period. Once the costs of revenue collection and/or work time are associated with the amounts collected, it is possible to derive cost of collection ratios and unit measures, such as, the unit cost of collection and amount collected per amount expended. (Interested readers can explore practical approaches to cost finding by consulting Joseph T. Kelley, *Costing Government Service: A Guide for Decision-making.* Chicago: Government Finance Officers Association, 1984.)

When applied, each cost concept provides a distinctive insight. Costs, variously calculated and arrayed, are not neutral in affect and effect, as the arrangement of data in budgets and financial statements has policy and managerial consequences. Consequently, budget officers must be knowledgeable about cost concepts and possess skill in their calculation and application.

We must further note that in those cases where cost centers do not satisfy the criteria listed in Exhibit 3.5, for example, no mathematical linkage between input and output, it is still desirable to support them with narratives providing factual information on mission, clientele, service standards, etc.

Significance. As organizing concepts, cost centers should focus attention on significant activities or purposes, especially those identified at the higher levels of aggregation. Testing a proposed aggregation for significance helps to discourage the proliferation of cost centers beyond those truly useful in budget formulation and execution - an ever present tendency. Testing for significance also helps to discourage the establishment of cost centers describing "instrumental" tasks, such as, reviewing applications, office housekeeping, conference attendance, inspections, etc., which provide organizing concepts for work plans, and, consequently, subsidiary accounting and performance records. Finally, testing cost centers for significance promotes format flexibility by encouraging the accountable officials to organize each annual budget to meet issues or topical needs.

To be deemed "significant," a programmatic cost center must serve two, or more, of the following purposes:

- To identify costs and work time for calculations of performance ratio calculations. Evidence of active management usage of performance ratios is required to justify cost center establishment for this purpose.

- To identify costs for periodic examination of significant resource mix options and/or alternative production techniques. Evidence of recent examination and resulting changes is required.

- To identify costs for service charge pricing. Evidence of such usage is required to justify cost center establishment for this purpose.

- To associate resources with organizational units and/or levels of supervision. Assignment of an accountable cost center manager is required to validate cost center establishment.

- To draw attention to outstanding problems/issues. To prompt this attention, costs can be

III. THE GRAMMAR OF BUDGETING

reassigned laterally and vertically to new issue-oriented cost center concepts. Conversely, in stable, efficient programs, cost center arrays can be compressed laterally and vertically by mergers and/or cost reassignments.

- To identify costs for aggregation and/or comparison with costs of similar functions in other cost center arrays. Evidence of decision-related usage of such aggregations and comparisons is required to validate the establishment of cost centers for this purpose.

- To organize and identify resource commitments for the implementation of salient policies. In these cases, the cost center array should be checked for excessive decomposition, as it may include more centers and levels than needed to confirm commitment.

- To isolate costs which cannot be easily or accurately assigned to other cost centers. Cost centers are justifiably used to isolate the "indirect," "fixed" or "common" costs of general supervision, central process units, sundry expenditures, "overhead" items, etc. Two or more cost centers in a peer group will probably require a "residual" cost center to isolate the common costs of supporting services and/or indirectly applied resources.

Format economy is a collateral, but secondary consideration. Compact arrays are preferred. Periodically updated, the chart of accounts should include no unused classifications and codes, especially the uniform classifications and codes applied to expenditure and revenue items. The coding scheme should include no unused digits. Frequently misapplied classifications and codes deserve corrective action and/or revision.

To satisfy this criterion for programmatic cost centers, at least 90% of the total array must meet the "significance" test.

Productivity. "Input" denotes applied resources. The cost of resources commonly represents, and measures, budget "input." Additionally, recognizing the importance of human effort in attaining budget goals, work time represents, and measures, budget "input." Other applied resources, such as, equipment, materials, electrical energy, etc., represent "input," but are less frequently used to calculate input/output ratios.

In order to be useful, a cost center must aggregate input which can be systematically related to performance indicators. The establishment of performance indicators requires management commitment and, often times, a willingness to accept less-than-perfect indicators. Even commonly used measures, such as "patient days" or "miles of road construction" can be criticized because these concepts may falsely suggest an unwarranted degree of uniformity of conditions and treatment. Obviously, it is easier to specify the output of fundamental tasks, than to do so at more inclusive levels of summarization. For example, the health concept, "Primary Care," may embrace many important activities, such as, maternal and child care, clinic services, health education, etc. By any test of significance, "Primary Care" qualifies as a cost center. But, as a cost center concept, "Primary Care" must also meet the performance linkage test, and, thus, input must be associated with a performance indicator, or, more appropriately in this case, an index of indicators associated with the activities subsumed by it.

The productivity criterion, linkage between applied resources and performance indicators. must be applied to all cost aggregations, and foregone only where conceptual and data aggregation problems prove insurmountable.

III. THE GRAMMAR OF BUDGETING

Necessarily, the calculation of performance ratios requires the measurement of performance and the maintenance of records. In theory, cost centers should embrace the cost of all resources applied to produce specified results. In practice, this rule is most likely to be applied to "direct," or "variable" costs, that is, those costs which are subject to an accountable manager's discretion. When they vary in amount or tempo, directly applied resources produce variances in results. If inclusive, and mathematically linked to performance measurements, a cost center embracing only "direct" or "variable" costs may be deemed satisfactory, other things being equal. Of the criteria defining a model budget, a mathematical linkage between input and performance measures should be given great weight in allocation decisions.

To satisfy the model criterion for the linkage between input and results, at least 75% of the total cost center array must, at minimum, strictly adhere to the "direct" or "variable" cost inclusion rule, and be mathematically linked to performance measures by ratios.

Accountability. To ensure accountability, every cost center must be assigned to a specific manager with sufficient power to be capable of meeting, and exceeding, performance targets. In order to provide the needed flexibility, cost center managers should be granted "lumpsum allotments" established by reference to work plans and subsequent performance reviews. Further, as indicated below, they should be empowered to certify payroll time, initiate purchase requisitions and certify invoices for payment. In contrast to some budget formats, which tend to diffuse responsibility, the model budget format places a premium on active management of costs and performance, each cost center representing a commitment of resources for the attainment of an estimated production target(s). As noted above, every cost center should be formally assigned to a cost center manager who is accountable for the behavior of both allocated resources and expected results. To qualify as an accountable cost center, its manager must be entrusted with a significant number of the following duties: 1) formulate cost center budgets, work plans and allotment requests,

2) re-allocate cost center budgets, when necessary, 3) maintain, monitor, report and actively use performance records, 4) supervise staff funded by the cost center, 5) discipline staff financed by the cost center, 6) certify work time and/or payrolls, 7) authorize requisitions and/or purchase orders, and 8) certify receipt of purchases/vendor payments.

Reportability. It has been widely observed that program officials attempting to formulate and implement results-oriented budgets are acutely dependent on the services of sympathetic, flexible accountants. This essential relationship is subject to the following considerations:

1. To avoid excessive accounting and reporting, each cost center should be tested for recording ease and accuracy. Complex cost allocations and extensive splitting of work time is necessary in some cases, but, as a rule, should be avoided.

2. Frequently, the work plans supporting particular cost centers will include an extensive array of activities and their associated unit costs and/or unit times, requiring the assignment, recording and reporting of costs and work hours by the designated activities. As a rule, subsidiary ledgers should be used for detailed work plan accounting, these ledgers to be maintained by the accountable cost center managers, but periodically reconciled to the main accounting records.

In general, the standards for recording and reporting revenues and expenditures are governed by well-established accounting conventions, supported by auditing procedures. The accumulation and reporting of performance data must also be subject to conventions which guarantee validity and reliability. As noted above in the discussion of the linkage between applied resources and results, the formal integration of input

III. THE GRAMMAR OF BUDGETING

and performance data is regarded as the essential characteristic of results-oriented budgeting.

Therefore, standards governing the collection and reporting of performance data, are as important as the standards for controlling and reporting payrolls and other disbursements (the input), and should also be regularly audited.

Subject to the above considerations, the accounting staff should 1) promptly record the revenue, disbursement reservations and disbursements, as assigned to cost centers by the chart of accounts, and 2) periodicaly audit and evaluate the subsidiary ledgers maintained for work plan accounting, including the records of cost center performance data.

To satisfy the criterion for accounting and reporting, at least 90% of receipts, disbursement reservations and disbursements must be recorded on the day following deposit or authorization, respectively. Additionally, 90% of work plan records should be audited at least once per year.

Acceptance. Obviously, the persons doing the work should understand and agree with the cost center concept, and support its productivity implications. It is equally obvious that acceptance cannot be left to chance because agency leaders vary in their willingness to consult constructively on the issues of cost center definition and specification of performance indicators. Managers at all levels should consult and collaborate. It is particularly important to involve overhead staff, and the staffs of centralized auxiliary services in the selection of cost centers and, especially, production targets, lest accountable cost center managers suffer from untimely delivery of essential supporting services.

As indicated, due to the importance of budget formats, budget officers are the accountable officials for the determination of revenue and expenditure classifications, subject, of course, to consultation with their jurisdiction's program leaders and accountants.

At this point, we must be quick to note that computer technology has made it possible for budget officers to reach beyond the traditional mono-value, hierarchical approach to "cross-classify" revenue and expenditure arrays, creating multiple perspectives. For example, a performance budget for a technical high school would display an array of cost centers listing allocations for teaching vocational skills, such as business, construction, graphic arts, health, etc. To provide greater insight into the school program, the document could also display a cross-classified cost center array assigning relevant portions of these allocations to the attainment of academic attainment. This is to support the point that many public programs serve more than one value or objective. By attaching different programmatic concepts to the same expenditure arrays, this enrichment of budget documentation promotes wider and deeper understandings of the nature and linkage of public policies. The technique of cross-classification is further explored at an appropriate point later on.

Computer technology has also made it far easier for officials to employ mathematical modeling in budget calculations. The role of mathematical modeling in the budget process is discussed in Part Five, *Formulation and Documentation Guidelines*.

Requirement: Format Elaboration and Flexibility

Before continuing, it may prove useful to reader to review the key points of this discussion about the importance of budgetary classification. Results-oriented budgets incorporate program and project investments displayed in "cost center" arrays, measures of intended results, and, most crucially, calculations concerning the *relationship* of program and project investments to measures of results. Consequently, officials wishing to work with the information so provided inevitably find themselves concerned with the composition and integrity of 1) "cost centers," a term applied to aggregations of money or effort applied to programs and projects and 2) related performance data. Depending on one's accounting philosophy, applied financial resources may be aggregated as disbursements, expenditures or expense. Effort identifies work-time designated as hours, days, weeks, months or years. Further, the composition and integrity of monetary aggregations rests on the appropriate

III. THE GRAMMAR OF BUDGETING

classification and faithful assignment of "costs," variously defined (direct, indirect, fixed, variable, etc), depending on one's management philosophy and evaluation purpose.

Concerns about classification composition and integrity apply to the establishment and maintenance of the cost center aggregations of performance budgeting, goal-oriented program budgeting and the decision packages required by zero-base budgeting. These concerns also apply to the more elaborate off-spring of program budgeting, the planning/programming/budgeting system. In those frequent cases where declared goals transcend existing organizational units, goal attainment requires coordinated efforts of more than one organizational unit. This multi-unit situation presents program managers, work unit supervisors, accountants and budget officers with recurring classification, coding and accountability issues. Computer technology provides a way to simplify the management of a coding system comprising many digits by assigning a single surrogate code to an interrelated string of code numbers, such as 01-2-3-2-2-3-01-101, displayed in Exhibit 3.2, *A Sample Classification and Code Scheme*. To assign a surrogate code, all strings in a classification and code system are arranged in hierarchical order, and numbered accordingly. For example, the string noted above might be the 100th in the sequential order of strings, thus, 100 could be made to "stand-in" for that string lodged in a computerized "look-up" table. Entering the surrogate code locates the relevant string for entry into the accounting system and other appropriate records with information associated with that string. Using surrogate codes reduce coding effort and the possibility of coding error in entering a long set of inter-related codes in computer files and documents.

The Technique of Cross-classification

The proponents of the planning/programming/budgeting system called attention to the advantages of cross-classification. Applying this concept, also known as cross-walking, budget officers can variously identify, assemble and exhibit allocations contributing to the attainment of a program concept or policy goal when the allocations are actually budgeted to disparate organizational units, or even other governments. Governments of general jurisdiction are usually organizationally and programmatically complex. Such jurisdictions undoubtedly fund many programs that contribute (directly and indirectly) to the attainment of more than one programmatic purpose. Cross-classifications direct attention to these latent functions. Additionally, the multiple perspectives provided by cross-classifications may reveal opportunities to reduce costs and/or improve effectiveness and efficiency, as disparate efforts contributing to a desired programmatic policy or goal may not be efficacious. Consider the following possibilities for multi-dimensional budgeting:

> A city budget, normally divided into functional classes of general government, public safety, community maintenance and development, health, education, parks and recreation, might be cross-classified by geography, within functions and aggregated for all functions by districts. The odds are that such a cross-classified allocation pattern will result in different patterns of expenditure than one based solely on functions and organization. Might not city leaders also benefit from examining an organizational budget (departments of police, public works, health, etc.) cross-classified by demography? Governments of general jurisdiction, regardless of size can apply this technique. Cross-classifications promote insight and understanding. A budget for the operation and maintenance of a park system could be classified in terms of its contribution to recreation opportunities, educational services, and crime prevention. Recreation expenditures can be recognized as play, social work and a contribution to reducing the incidence of juvenile delinquency. In addition to its economic impact, publicly subsidized day care can be classified and evaluated as child development, education and social service. And so it goes. Attaching different verbal symbols

III. THE GRAMMAR OF BUDGETING

to the same expenditure pattern tends to promote wider and deeper understandings of the nature and linkage of public policies.

Because public programs frequently involve more than one organizational unit within a government, the classification schemes employed in program budgets are more complicated than those needed by performance formats. Program budgeting brings organizationally segregated program components together in one summary.

Most budget officers agree that this budget approach is very effective for policy-making, but requires extraordinary coordination and collaboration, such arrangements crossing normal responsibility lines during budget formulation and implementation. Even if jurisdictions can not support program budgets with appropriate organizational arrangements, including accounting support, it is possible to formulate and monitor program budgets by using the "cross-classification," or "cross-walk," technique selectively, on an as-needed basis.

Exhibit 3.6 A Family Planning Program Perspective

IMPACTS >	Maintaining Current Practitioners	Recruiting Lapsed Practitioners	Recruiting New Practitioners	Total
Family Planning Board	3,423.2	615.6	3575.2	7,614.0
Ministry of Health	3,000.0	75.4	835.5	3910.9
Ministry of Education			392.3	392.3
Youth/Community Development			1,107.6	1,107.6
Ministry of Agriculture	82.3		400.0	482.3
Total Cost	6,505.5	691.0	6,310.6	13,507.1
Number of Acceptors	114,000	20,000	43,000	177,000
Cost per Acceptor	57.06	34.55	146.76	76.31
Estimated Births				61,000
Estimated Births Averted				17,700
Cost per Averted Birth				763.31

An example of a cross-classified budget is displayed by Exhibit 3.6, *A Family Planning Program Perspective*. The program involved a coordinating agency, the Family Planning Board (FPB), and four ministries, including the key delivery system provided by the Ministry of Health through its extensive Maternal and Child Health Clinic System. For management purposes, within the FPB and the ministries, family planning was identified and coded as an array of cost centers. Additionally, using the "cross-classification," or "cross-walk" technique, the FPB budget officer prepared a program perspective summarizing the entire family planning budget, including all participating units of government. As shown in Exhibit 3.6, this Program Perspective cross-classified the allocations to the participating institutions to indicate their relative impact on the three key operating thrusts of the program.

With the availability of computer technology, the cross-classifications required to support program budgeting can be produced by reference to codes assigned for that purpose, designated, as needed, for analysis and/or decisions. Computer technology makes it possible to formulate and implement budgets with multiple formats. In contrast to mono-value formats, cross-classified formats permit policy officials to explore more than one dimensions of an expenditure proposal, facilitating insight and understanding.

In sum, cross-classifications encourage participants in the budget process to explore multiple dimensions of an expenditure pattern, highlighting and emphasizing the relationships potentially and actually present in public programs. Budget officers serving in jurisdictions relying on mono-value, hierarchical classification systems are advised to construct cross-classifications to direct attention to the multiple dimensions and benefits of various programs, and to help rationalize allocations. All budget officers should promote the use of cross-classification, made readily available via computer technology, which can provide the required coding and data assembly and display capabilities.

III. THE GRAMMAR OF BUDGETING

Further Thoughts on the Significance of Form and Procedure

It can be argued that budgets and budget procedures have become the key instruments of governance. If so, this marks a signal development in the sweep of history because political thinkers have generally held that the making of laws by accountable legislators and the faithful execution thereof by accountable executives was the essence of proper government. However, even if we discount speculation about the relative primacy of budgeting vs. lawmaking as public policy vehicles, the centrality of budgeting in contemporary governments is undeniable. Further, as the stakes grew, so did a perception that the forms and procedures of budgeting influence budgetary outcomes, that is, the process, itself, can not be regarded as an impartial instrument of policy. Giving this perception due weight, since the end of World War II countless officials have tried various results-oriented alternatives to the traditional Line-Item form of budgeting (LIB). Their efforts to employ results-oriented budgeting have met with varying degrees of acceptance, enthusiasm and success in a variety of jurisdictions throughout the United States, including its Federal Government, and, increasingly, the world. In assessing this experience, one must admire the tenacity of numberless officials, who, despite manifest difficulties and disappointments, kept striving to bring the benefits of results-oriented budgeting to their jurisdictions. As evidence of this tenacity, pursuant to the adoption of the Government Performance and Results Act, 1993, officials of the United States Government are currently making yet another attempt to install the prototypical form of results-oriented budgeting, namely Performance Budgeting (PerB).

By advancing a new way of channeling budgetary thought and action, the introduction of PerB, the earliest systematic alternative to LIB, stimulated thinking about the potential impact of alternative formats and procedures on policy and management decisions. As is well known, this led to the development of three additional alternatives to Line-Item Budgeting, and to each other, namely, Program Budgeting (ProB), the Planning, Programming, Budgeting System (PPBS) and Zero-Base Budgeting (ZBB). Although they differ in procedural detail, all four alternatives to Line-Item Budgeting encourage officials to specify relationships between applied resources and results. Importantly, however, the advocates of these alternatives to LIB directed attention to the novel resource allocation features of their favored approaches, slighting the necessities of budget execution, especially the requirements of appropriate administrative and accounting support. To this day, accountable officials have not satisfactorily addressed the implementation issues of results-oriented budgeting. The generally weak response to the implementation challenge of results-oriented budgeting is de facto recognition of manifest hazards and intrinsic difficulties.

By directly associating agency appropriations with input summaries (personal services, non-personal expense, etc.) or objects of expenditure (salaries, electrical charges, etc.), Line-Item Budgeting provides clear accountability for estimates, procurement, encumbrances and disbursements. Referencing commodity classifications and codes, assigned personnel can accurately charge payments for personal services, commodities and contractual services to appropriate line-item budget allocations.

Although acknowledging these virtues, critics rightly point out that LIB formats and procedures do not explicitly draw attention to performance accountability. Obviously, even though they may be working with Line-Item Budgets, public officials are continuously concerned with performance. However, the format and procedures of the typical Line-Item Budget do not require them to systematically calculate, document and maintain specific relationships between applied resources, production techniques and results, variously defined

III. THE GRAMMAR OF BUDGETING

as output/outcome/impact variables. Given the seemingly remorseless growth of public services throughout the world, this shortcoming is a serious deficiency. Hence, the abiding interest in forms of budgeting which relate allocated resources to results, despite manifest hazards and intrinsic difficulties of implementation.

Although many government jurisdictions make financial information electronically available to the public, they customarily publish the budgets submitted for legislative consideration and adoption in book form. Of course, the budgeting approach adopted by any given jurisdiction determines the layout of expenditure displays in published budget books. However, discounting this textual imperative, thousands of budget books published annually throughout North America vary significantly in form and substance, evidence that the budget officers assigned to design and produce these documents exercise literary imagination.

Because they enrich the budget process with performance data and programmatic interpretations, jurisdictions practicing results-oriented approaches provide the budget officers charged with budget book design and production an abundance of text which can be associated with expenditure and revenue arrays. By way of example, Exhibit 3.7, *Elements of a Model Performance Budget,* provides an indicative illustration of text supporting a performance style budget.

Budgetary Thought for Budget Officers

EXHIBIT 3.7 Elements of a Model Performance Budget

ECONDARY EDUCATION
Technical High School

		BUDGET
1	**COST CENTER**	
	Auto/Aero/Power	1,200,000
	Business	420,000
	Construction	480,000
	Electrical/Electronic	720,000
	Graphic Arts	1,020,000
	Health Services	240,000
	Mechanical Trades	1,300,000
	Services	629,000
	Total	6,000,000
2	**FUNDING PLAN**	
	State Aid	2,000,000
	Industry and Business Grants	4,500,000
	Property Taxes	(500,000)
	Total	6,000,000
3	**ESTIMATED BENEFITS**	
	Personal Satisfaction	+ but ?
	Diffusion of Knowledge	+ but ?
	Broadened Options	+ but ?
	P.V. Extra Income Per Student	85,140

TARGETS. This budget funds 1500 students, 83% of total applicants, lowest ratio in Tech history. See the Five-Year Forecast for a discussion of this problem. Achievement ratios are rising, but under expectations.

LAST YEAR	THIS YEAR	INDICATOR	BUDGET
80	85	% Above Reading Norm	90
75	80	% Above Math Norm	85
90	92	Atendance Ratio	95
85	87	Graduation Ratio	90

As also noted, the graduation and attendance ratios, estimated to improve his year, are set higher next year. The marginal cost of attaining targets is estimated at $100,000 in computer expense and extra counseling. Curriculum design is based on annual surveys of skill demand in the community, and alumni "feedback." The distribution of resources to the School's dual objectives is displayed by the cross-classification.

III. THE GRAMMAR OF BUDGETING

Exhibit 3.7 Continued

COST CENTER	ACADEMIC ATTAINMENT	VOCATIONAL ATTAINMENT
Auto/Aero/Power	480,000	720,000
Business	170,000	250,000
Construction	190,000	290,000
Electric/Electronic	290,000	430,000
Graphic Arts	410,000	610,000
Health Services	100,000	140,000
Mechanical Trades	520,000	780,000
Services	250,000	370,000
	2,410,000	3,590,000
Number of Students	1,500	1,500
Unit Cost	$1,607	$2,393

INTERPRETING ESTIMATED BENEFITS. Graduates are expected to add an estimated average of $10,000 to their annual income during the first 20 years after graduation. This incomes stream has a present value (PV) of $85,140, discounted at 10%. The public's investment in the average graduate is currently estimated at $16,000. After age 16, students contribute their time, measured by foregone earnings, estimated at an average of $10,000. Thus, the investment, private and public, in a technical education is estimated to total $26,000. Subtracting this investment from $85,140 yields a net present value (NPV) of $59,140 attributable to the Technical High program. Additional benefits are listed. The notation "+ but?" indicates that these benefits are deemed positive, but are of unknown value

MARGINAL PRODUCTIVITY. The academic attainment budget is up $100,000, balanced by a decrease of the budget for vocational attainment. In the opinion of the faculty, this shift will not reduce their ability to reach the indicated targets.

FIVE-YEAR FORECAST. Holding unit costs constant, the budget may be expected to rise by $400,000 each year to accommodate enrollment to 1,800 students, the design capacity of the school

	BUDGET	STUDENT ENROLLMENT
Budget	$6,000,000	1,500
Future Year Two	6,400,000	1,600
Future Year Three	6,800,000	1,700
Future Year Four	7,200,000	1,800
Future Year Five	7,200,000	1,800

Budgetary Thought for Budget Officers

Funding a technical high school, the model budget incorporates 1) a section allocating proposed investment (expenditures), presented in cost center order, 2) a funding plan balanced to the proposed investment, 3) an array listing estimated benefits accruing to the proposed investment, and 4) a commentary. This commentary includes a performance data array presenting targets, a "cross classification" linking programmatic cost centers to education purposes, and unit cost calculations. These arrays are accompanied by an interpretive text.

Allocations are the most fundamental part of budget documents, in this case $6,000,000, decomposed into a set of "cost centers." Although not revealed by this array, each cost center is a summary of costs to be charged to subsidiary aggregations of expenditure. Expressive terms are used to classify the costs, conveying expenditure purpose.

The Funding Plan identifies assigned resources by source. As expenditure must be funded or financed, the total of revenue (or receipts in case of finance) shown in this data array must equal or exceed the allocation. In those cases where revenues attributed to the activities supported by the allocation exceed the resource requirement, the excess should be shown negatively and assigned to the Funding Plan of another allocation. In this case, the revenue from state aid and grants from benefiting private enterprises exceeds the allocation, reducing the need for an assignment of the jurisdiction's general revenue, namely property taxes.

The third data array provides information on likely benefits logically attributed to the Technical High program. Ideally, the estimated value of attributed benefits should equal or exceed program cost. In those cases where benefits can not be monetized (a common aspect of public programs and projects), one can indicate the tendency of an identified benefit, positive or negative, and the fact that its value is unknown, by the following shorthand:

"+ but ?," or " – but ?"

III. THE GRAMMAR OF BUDGETING

The commentary should provide insight into program rationale, including references to the principal issues, problems or opportunities addressed by the budget allocation. Performance data arrays should be associated with this part of the commentary. The skill-oriented cost center array is cross-classified by educational objectives to highlight the dual values pursued by the Technical High School faculty. This cross-classification isolates portions of the allocation for the display of relative unit costs and the discussion of marginal productivity. The commentary on Estimated Benefits provides insight into key assumptions and calculations, and encourages discussion of investment returns.

Although the data array displaying the skill-based cost centers does not show historical comparisons, it is sometimes useful to refer to current and prior year experience, as does the discussion of Marginal Productivity. . The Five-Year Forecast serves to bring the future into the present, alerting budget reviewers and policymakers to possible implications of budget commitments and emerging program issues, problems and opportunities. .

Reflecting my experience, composing budget books incorporating narrative text, such as that presented by Exhibit 3.7, is a challenging task for assigned budget officers. In particular, given the rationale for their utilization, results-oriented budgets require the application of literary and communications criteria, which require the subordination of accounting arrays to prominent and coordinated placement of interpretative texts and tables. For a discussion of applicable criteria, see my essay, "Budgets as Literature," included in *Effective Budgetary Presentations: The Cutting Edge*. Compiled by Gerald Miller, Municipal Finance Officers Association, 1982.

IV. ACCOUNTING FOUNDATIONS

Paradoxically, the evidence, to date, indicates that many governments have been willing to introduce results-oriented budgeting, but have been slow or unwilling to support the introduction with appropriate administrative and accounting arrangements, condemning the enterprise to superficiality, if not outright failure. With specific reference to budgetary accounting, knowledgeable officials, especially experienced budget officers, trace the failure to effectively practice results-oriented budgeting to accounting deficiencies. It is beyond doubt that collateral changes in the supporting institutional arrangements must complement the installation of the various alternatives to Line-Item Budgeting. Significantly, in the United States, the provisions of the 1996 Federal Financial Management Improvement Act support the latest attempt to install Performance Budgeting by requiring federal agencies to install management accounting. Although progress is reportedly lagging, the injunction to provide appropriate accounting support gives this newest effort a fighting chance to succeed, in contrast to previous attempts to install various forms of results-oriented budgeting without devoting sufficient attention to the administrative and accounting conditions of success.

Accounting Essentials

In every jurisdiction, accounting capabilities and performance condition the use of the appropriation process as an instrument of public policy and management. In short, budgets and budgeting depend on accounting for organizational lodgment and programmatic effect. This axiom is widely appreciated, even where accounting support for budgeting practice falls far short of its potential. Accounting support for the appropriation process not only varies significantly among governments across the world, but, tends to be limited to the bare essentials of expenditure recording and control. In recent decades, financial accounting and reporting has attracted critical attention, with significant results. As governments with sub-standard financial accounting and reporting are not likely to be providing strong accounting support for budgeting, budget officers have welcomed improvements in financial accounting and reporting. Given the centrality of the appropriation process in the formulation and implementation of public policy, accounting support for budgeting also deserves critical attention — and investment.

Budgetary accounting is a form of management accounting. As such, the provision of accounting support for budget formulation and implementation is not subject to the same type of authoritative standards increasingly applied to the practice of financial accounting and reporting, public and private, throughout the world. Consequently, government jurisdictions are free to determines the extent of their management accounting practice, and by implication, its accounting support for budgeting. The following discussion explores accounting support problems in sufficient detail to identify desiderata which might be used to define a satisfactory model of budgetary accounting.

The Evolving Accounting Environment

Encouraged by multi-lateral international organizations, and also responding to the information requirements of an integrating global economy, governments throughout the world strive to upgrade and standardize their financial accounting and reporting. Because budget processes are strongly conditioned by accounting methodology and staff capabilities, the adoption of upgraded and standardized financial

IV. ACCOUNTING FOUNDATIONS

accounting and reporting has been good news for officials interested in the practice of results-oriented budgeting. However, experience, to date, indicates that this movement, by itself, does not guarantee that governments are willing to install and maintain the additional administrative and accounting institutions required for the effective practice of results-oriented budgeting.

When derived from standardized financial accounts, independently audited reports can usually provide reliable information about an organization's financial status. Although government officials find standard-based financial reports useful, to outside interested parties, these reports are absolutely indispensable. For this reason, the major multi-lateral international organizations – International Monetary Fund, United Nations and World Bank– have consistently encouraged the adoption of standardized financial accounting and reporting by the governments of the world, stressing the inter-related values of transparency, disclosure and comparability. For the same reason, representatives of the influential investment community have encouraged the adoption of Generally Accepted Accounting Principles (GAAP) by public and private organizations seeking access to the world's capital markets. Responding to these authoritative recommendations, the number of governments practicing standardized financial accounting and reporting, or striving to do so, has been slowly increasing. Given the availability of GAAP-based financial accounting computer software, and the spur supplied by the continuing advance of global economic integration, one may safely predict the eventual standardization of government financial accounting and reporting throughout the world.

In contrast, the constituency for management accounting lies inside, rather than outside organizations. Organizations use well-known accounting concepts and procedures to record and report information useful to their managers. This extension of accounting practice beyond that required for financial accounting and reporting is not currently subject to authoritative, GAAP-like requirements.

Consequently, every organization is free to determine the scope and subject matter of its management accounting program. Although not authoritatively standardized, management accounting is a distinct field of knowledge, supported by literature and formal coursework in educational institutions. Centered on costs, aggregated and evaluated by product and/or management responsibility, enterprise managers throughout the world make extensive use of management accounting. However, excepting their public enterprises, governments have been reluctant to support their public service programs with management accounting. Within the United States, initiatives affecting governmental accounting began in 1934. In a seminal move, the Municipal Finance Officers Association of the United States and Canada (MFOA) issued the first of its influential series of manuals (known as "blue books") embracing the recommendations of the then newly established National Committee on Governmental Accounting (NCGA) for the improvement of government accounting. Several of these recommendations directly and indirectly affected the accounting-budgeting relationship. NCGA suggestions included 1) establishment of a set of separate, but interrelated, "funds" as the basic accounting organization of governmental jurisdictions, 2) adoption of the "double entry" accounting methodology, 3) incorporation of budgetary accounts as an integral component of governmental accounting systems, and 4) recognition of expenditures and revenues on a "modified accrual" basis, except for governmental enterprises which were advised to use the accrual approach.

A notable enhancement of governmental accounting within the United States followed the virtual bankruptcy of New York City in 1974. In response to this event, a broad-based movement, strongly supported by the Government Finance Officers Association (GFOA, formerly MFOA), successfully effected a major change in the utility of governmental accounting by establishing "disclosure" and "transparency" as controlling purposes. Although not focused on government, the United States Government reacted similarly to major corporate scandals by adopting the Public Company Accounting and Investor Protection Act of 2002.

In 1984, the Governmental Accounting Standards Board (GASB) replaced the NCGA. Summing up at this point, after nearly

IV. ACCOUNTING FOUNDATIONS

a century of effort, adherence to the standards adopted by the NCGA-GASB has increased significantly within the United States. An important exception to this general adherence concerns requirements for the maintenance of proper fixed asset records. This is regrettable as such records are not only useful in considering capital investment policy, but also facilitate the allocation of capital charges to operating cost centers. It is also regrettable that, despite the heavy promotion of various forms of results-oriented budgeting during the period, requisite accounting support requirements did not receive proper attention.

Accumulating experience indicates that the effectiveness of results-oriented budgeting (defined as the efficient attainment of performance objectives) depends on management's success in employing a series of implementation instruments. Employed sequentially, the suggested series embraces four instruments of budget implementation: 1) work plans, 2) allotments, 3) periodic formal performance reviews and 4) timely corrective action. Effectively, these instruments must be supported by a) an elaborate, flexible classification and coding scheme and b) accounting procedures facilitating the formal integration of non-monetary performance data and monetary accounting data.

If implemented dynamically, as recommended, this four-phase monitoring sequence enables accountable officials to recognize and diagnose allocation and performance problems in time to take appropriate corrective action before the given reporting period ends. Obviously, the ability of officials to take effective corrective action within any given reporting period is critically dependant on timely recording and reporting of accounting and performance data. The role of timing cannot be overstressed, for it is timely corrective action by accountable officials that provides results-oriented budgeting with its managerial muscle. Considering the importance of goal attainment for effective results-oriented budgeting, monitoring systems that do not provide timely recording, reporting and corrective action are fatally deficient. Sadly, at the present time (2015), the typical budget monitoring system tends to rest on "after-the-period" reporting, when the opportunity to alter a likely undesired outcome has passed - forever!

Indispensability of Accounting Leadership

As noted above, the accounting support for the recommended monitoring sequence should include a) an elaborate, flexible classification and coding scheme and b) accounting procedures facilitating the formal integration of non-monetary performance data and monetary accounting data. Translated into leadership principles, these imperatives require a willingness to 1) make the chart of accounts serve programmatic as well as control purposes, 2) use accounting procedures and records to systematically relate non-monetary performance data to monetary accounting data, and 3) establish and maintain reporting practices that keep financial and productivity data flowing to all program units, validated, consolidated and made available on a timely basis. Specifically, the design and operation of the accounting system should satisfy the following criteria:

- To provide for the recording and reporting of budgetary transactions, accounting procedures should incorporate budgetary accounts, recording estimated revenue, appropriations, allocations and allotments, recording revenue as received and commitments and disbursements as incurred. .

- To maintain control of the budget during its execution, accounting procedures should subtract commitments (contingent liabilities, encumbrances, reservations) and disbursements from

IV. ACCOUNTING FOUNDATIONS

appropriate appropriation/allotment amounts, indicating the uncommitted balance available to support additional commitments and disbursements. (Modified Accrual)

- To encourage disbursement planning, and by implication, program planning, appropriations and allotments for operations and maintenance should lapse, unless committed by purchase order, at the end of allotment periods, if allotments are used, and most certainly at the end of the fiscal period. Project appropriations (additions to fixed assets), regarded as no-year appropriations, should continue to be valid until project completion.

- To facilitate periodic performance reviews, the accounting system should incorporate "accounts" for recording and reporting performance data in cost center order, specifically, work hours, other evidences of effort, and associated performance indicators and ratios. It is especially important that the accounting system clearly distinguish between "control" and "analysis" classifications and codes by permitting expenditure control to be identified with a programmatic classification and code, rather than expenditure items. For clarification of this point, consult Exhibit 3.3, *A Classification and Code Scheme*. Consistent with the "performance" budgeting concept of managerial accountability, Code Level 6 would likely be identified as a control code. It would identify a "lumpsum" or "global" allotment, and, thus, the point where the accounting controller stops further expenditure exceeding the allotment. Levels 7 and 8 function as analytical codes, useful for identifying expenditures for the purposes of evaluation and cost estimation. With reference to expenditure controls, their location within a cascade of classifications and their associated codes is an important, and contentious, issue. In each jurisdiction, the resolution of this issue determines the fundamental design of its expenditure ledger. If the control points are associated with results-oriented "lump-sum" summaries (program, project, activity or task), rather than with major object summaries or objects of expenditure, these latter entries will serve as analytical rather than control identifiers and codes, providing information only. As noted in Part 3, in those governments where the leading officials are unwilling to establish controls at a programmatic level (lump-sum), the managerial assumptions of results-oriented budgeting are seriously compromised.

- To avoid understatements, all expenditure and revenue should be aggregated and reported in gross, rather than net terms.

- To maximize its usefulness, accounting and performance data should be recorded accurately and reported at times required for the effective conduct of the performance review phases of the budget monitoring sequence.

IV. ACCOUNTING FOUNDATIONS

Failure to satisfy all six criteria must be regarded as a most serious lapse, having pervasive, deleterious consequences for all dimensions of the budgetary process. It is instructive (and sobering) to note that accounting professionals clearly perceived the potential impact of results-oriented budgeting on accounting procedures. The following comment in 1954 by James M. Cunningham, a Certified Public Accountant and a former president of the Municipal Finance Officers Association (MFOA) may be taken as representative:

> "The adoption of the performance budget by a municipality requires a major change in accounting procedures in order to develop the possibilities of the new method to the fullest advantage." Accounting Publication Series, 11-2, MFOA, May 1, 1954.

Ideally, results-oriented budgeting is most appropriately supported by management accounting procedures. Without doubt, management accounting, tied to a standardized financial accounting system, provides the ideal form of accounting support for results-oriented budgeting. It offers the best way to calculate and document reasonable approximations of the "true" cost of attaining given government objectives. Generally, in the past, governments have been notably reluctant to support results-oriented budgeting procedures with comprehensive management accounting systems which continuously track and report total costs. It seemed just too complicated and expensive, and unless associated with strong results-oriented administrative institutions, will appear to everyone to be a waste of time and money. Consequently, lacking management accounting support, officials interested in employing results-oriented budgeting must be content to establishing relationships between performance indicators and direct costs.

Most assuredly, "performance" style budgeting, which, in theory, features "lumpsum" allotments to "cost centers," such allotments to be executed via detailed work plans and periodic performance reviews, requires a great deal of cooperation from governmental accountants. Consequently, governments wishing to install results-oriented budgeting, or those seeking to do it better, are well-advised to first ensure that requisite accounting foundations are in place and working smoothly. The attainment of appropriate accounting support is only possible when a jurisdiction's leading finance officials identify with the problems of programmatic and project goal attainment. However, strong forces work against the expression of a programmatic orientation by finance leaders in every government. Characteristically, finance leaders tend to identify budgeting as a problem of financial "control," and, therefore, define the role of accounting in budgeting negatively and narrowly. According to this line of thinking, budget implementation is accounting, pure and simple. Government leaders subscribing to this philosophy tend to ignore and/or devalue the connection of accounting arrangements to other procedures which assist management in attaining the programmatic and project purposes of budgeting. Clearly, in governments where the financial control mindset is dominant, the introduction and maintenance of recommended procedures focused on programmatic and project goal attainment will not rest on strong institutional foundations

To be fair, even if willing, many government accounting units frequently lack the capability to put in place and consistently maintain appropriate budgetary accounting and reporting. When compared with the demands of financial accounting, results-oriented budgeting imposes additional operating burdens on the accounting staff:

- Accounts and classifications proliferate, including identification of fixed and variable costs.

- Transactions and entries increase in number and complexity.

IV. ACCOUNTING FOUNDATIONS

- Reconciliation problems increase.

- Accounting reports display fewer continuities as accounts and classifications change from period to period to meet changing issues. (This situation may also result in demands for restatement of accounting data to illuminate new issues.)

- Accountants and auditors are given increased responsibility for the entry and integrity of "non-dollar" data (work load, performance indicators and program benefit information) and the calculation of relationships of this data to expenditure and revenue information.

Notwithstanding the difficulties cited above, it is encouraging to note that many governments are increasing led by officials who understand and support the selected use of the concepts of "management" accounting, including cost centers and concepts of performance measurement. If integrated with supporting administrative institutions, management accounting can provide a solid foundation for the introduction of results-oriented budgeting, provided that the financial accounting system incorporates expenditure and revenue ledgers which permit the maintenance of an elaborate, flexible scheme of cost centers that can reach the lowest levels of supervision throughout the government organization. With this capability, every supervisor can function as a "cost center manager," accountable for the behavior of work time, variable (controllable) costs, related revenues, and, most important, performance. As a practical matter, the introduction and maintenance of results-oriented budgeting, with its heavy demands on the accounting system, cannot be accomplished without the leadership and enthusiastic support of governmental finance officers, especially accountants.

At the time of this writing (2015), efforts to improve government performance were underway in the United States, including an effort by the Obama administration to identify and remedy outstanding problems and invigorate the existing federal government performance system. Performance reporting by state and local governments has attracted the concern of the Government Accounting Standards Board (GASB), which developed guidelines for voluntary reporting of service efforts and accomplishments. In a collateral (but independent) effort, a coalition of eleven public interest groups, working though a National Performance Management Commission, staffed by GFOA, developed a framework for performance management for state and local governments. It is noteworthy that these efforts focus on the collection, use and dissemination of performance data, assuming, rather than addressing, the accounting requirements of results-oriented budgeting.

V. FORMULATION and DOCUMENTATION GUIDELINES

Does the manner of budgeting determine who gets what? Variously phased, this question enlivened the thinking of budget officers (and many others) since 1949, when the Commission on Organization of the Executive Branch of Government, popularly known as the Hoover Commission, recommended that the United States Government adopt Performance Budgeting (PerB). This proposed break with tradition initiated experimentation with various alternative budget formats and associated procedures. Although they differ in format and procedures, each alternative to Line-Item Budgeting (LIB) rested on the belief that budget formats and procedures influence budget decisions — evidence favoring an affirmative answer to our opening question. Further, many budget officers perceived the resistance of sundry entrenched interests to the implementation of these alternatives as providing conclusive testimony confirming the influence of format and procedures on budgetary outcomes.

Despite the hypocrisy and vagaries of political life, public officials are known to respond to the presentation of evidence and logic (not always in ways recommended by budget officers, to be sure). Consequently, the organization of budget documentation is never a trivial matter. Many respected students of budgeting have emphasized the importance of data organization and interpretation. As previously noted, Jesse Burkhead, in the Preface to his classic, "*Government Budgeting*,"1956, stated that, "the way in which revenue and expenditure are grouped for decision-making is the most important aspect of budgeting." Two years before, in

"*Program Budgeting* (1954), Frederick C. Mosher thoroughly explored the impact of budget structure on programming and budgeting in the Department of the Army. Evidently, if we want to encourage in-depth thinking about programmatic and financial implications of budget decisions, we must look critically at the way budgets are composed and communicated.

> **Consequently, thinking in terms of our subject matter, budget officers should ever strive to nourish official and citizen thought about the intrinsic and relative merits of budget allocations — the defining questions of budget evaluation. Guided by this purpose, budget officers are never wrong in creating pertinent data arrays and cogent interpretations, thereof, as prominent features of the budget process.**

As the custodians of the budget process, budget officers are usually responsible for the design of budget formulation formats and procedures. The budget officers so assigned become metaphysicians of a sort, as the resulting forms and instructions define the reality of budgeting for participants in the process. Working within the textual framework established by budget officers, program officials supply estimates and interpretative text. With reference to the document submitted to appropriation authorities, budget officers are usually responsible for the estimates and any supporting text. In the typical jurisdiction, its chief executive initiates the process of budget documentation by issuing a "call" for the formulation of estimates for the upcoming budget period. The process ends with editing required to record the budget decisions of the jurisdiction's appropriation authority. The documentation requirements of budget implementation are explored in Part Eight, *Implementation Methodology: Dynamic Monitoring*.

In bureaucracies, superiors usually obtain desired information from subordinates, in form, if not substance. This expected reflex action

V. FORMULATION and DOCUMENTATION GUIDELINES

empowers budget officers, who usually have the duty to express the jurisdiction's principles of budget formulation and documentation in the text of the call for estimates. Consequently, the information provided by program officials is strongly influenced by the selected budget format, formulation instructions and documentation requirements. To be sure, regardless of format, line-item type categories, (salaries, commodities, contracts, etc.) invariably lie at the base of every expenditure classification system. Line item categories facilitate the estimating process, but may not be prominently displayed, if at all, in the text explaining and justifying proposed allocations.

Assuming complete reliance on a line-item format, program officials are typically asked to identify the costs which make the difference between estimated current and upcoming year expenditure. This information centers attention on incremental changes, rather than on the merits of current year expenditure, commonly known as the "base."

Each of the alternative budget approaches features a distinct method of aggregating and identifying estimates. As briefly characterized below, each approach provides a different version of budget "reality:"

> If a performance format, accountable officials are asked to quantify the work to be done or targets to be attained, by means of aggregations of expenditure, identified as functions, activities, tasks or projects.

> If a program format, accountable officials are asked to specify goals to be attained through a requested expenditure aggregation identified by programmatic classifications, sometimes mixed with organizational identifiers.

> If a zero-based format, without reference to prior or current year data, accountable officials are asked to aggregate and prioritize variously classified proposed expenditures, presented as "decision packages."

It is important to note that, when adopted, a government budget represents a kind of "contract" between policymakers and administrators. Because budget documents embody certain understandings about future official behavior, they should satisfy literary, accounting and public relations standards. Bringing the form and content of budget documents under critical review involves several considerations:

> First, budget documents should be compact and readable. Budget-makers should avoid abstract language and minutiae, and they should test all exhibits and commentary for relevance. In addition, they should provide significant facts rather than generalizations. From a literary point of view, a good budget permits legislators and citizens to grasp its service and goal-attainment implications without having to refer to other sources. The rule of relevance is often ignored. Performance data arrays are frequently carried forward from year to year, showing unexplained variations in work loads and goal attainment. Furthermore, these variations often are not related to variations in associated expenditures and revenues. And, in a disturbing number of cases, performance data are aggregated on a calendar-year basis in a budget for a different fiscal period, making it impossible to strike a unit cost to relate expenditures to work loads or performance goals.

> Second, the budget maker's skill in topic selection and emphasis determines the literary quality of the budget documents. One should not slavishly reproduce the chart of accounts in public budget documents, nor standardize it from year-to-year, both of which are widespread vices. Expenditure and revenue arrays should relate to defined issues, problems and opportunities, rather than to organizational units or accounting charts. Obviously, if a budget is to relate to issues, problems and opportunities, its

V. FORMULATION and DOCUMENTATION GUIDELINES

organization must be flexible, particularly in the structure of expenditure and revenue titles. As conditions change from year to year, so must the format. It should also be noted that the structure of the titles determines the number of performance exhibits and commentaries, and thus the size and content of the budget document.

Third, every data array deserves interpretation. This rule ensures the formal relationship of expenditures and revenues to work loads and performance targets. Unfortunately, this rule is not firmly established. As a result, budget documents frequently contain page after page of tabular material on expenditures and performance that do not include explanations or interpretations.

Finally, the format and content of published budgets (including those made available on-line) influence the format and content of the supporting records and procedures, as well as the quality of budgetary thought. By using formats appropriately, document designers can help to diffuse the literary ideals of good budgeting throughout an organization.

Standardized information helps to facilitate the appraisal of the intrinsic and relative merit of proposed allocations. The specified topics should cause budget requesters to think critically, that is, use evidence and logic in the analysis of program rationale, goal specification, the evaluation of program results, and the examination of expenditure, workload and revenue relationships.

As listed in Exhibit 5.1, the recommended documentation should 1) define the issues, problems and opportunities to be attacked programmatically; 2) state goals in practical, measurable, time-bound terms; 3) identify collaborators and affected parties; 4) identify conditions required for goal attainment; 5) reference written work plans for executing the preferred problem solution(s); 6) display budget allocations in a results-oriented (rather than commodity) format; 7) identify alternatives considered, but rejected, and why.

Exhibit 5.1 Formulation Topics and Documentation

	STATEMENT	SPECIFICATIONS
1	RATIONALE	A concise statement of the perplexity(ies) to be addressed, defined as issues, problems and opportunities justifying the budget. Identifies causal relationships (correlations) between key variables and desired results. .
2	GOAL(S)	As targets, performance indicators are defined in practical, measurable, time-bound terms.
3	COLLABORATORS AND AFFECTED PARTIES	In addition to units providing (upstream) or receiving (downstream) assistance from the unit in question, identifies those to be served and/or regulated by the proposed activities, providing insight into the conferred benefits. .
4	CONDITIONS OF PERFORMANCE	Description of factors required to produce goal attainment. These include institutional aspects (organization, procedures, staff capability, regulations, procedures, equipment, etc.), and most important, the assumptions and standards which influence the size, shape, direction and feasibility of proposed programmatic solution to the situation described in Statement #1.
5	WORK PLAN (Preferred Solution)	A two-part statement reflecting the preferred solution to the situation described in Statement 1. The first part provides a matrix, listing activities or tasks, assigned work hours allocated by time periods or milestones, and pertinent performance ratios, such as output per work hour or unit costs. The second part provides a commentary relating the planned work to Statements 1, 2 and 3.
6	BUDGET	Supporting the preferred solution, a proposed "balanced" budget displays cost centers, performance data and interpretation.
7	ALTERNATIVES	A concise description of programmatic options considered, but rejected in favor of a preferred solution supported by a proposed work plan and allocation. Considerations include objectives, mix of resources and production techniques. These options should include at least one lower and one higher cost alternative to the recommended allocation, including the estimated impact on performance indicators.

V. FORMULATION and DOCUMENTATION GUIDELINES

The suggested topology confers four benefits. First, requiring accountable program managers to address each of these interrelated topics provides budget authorities with assurance that the requested allocation has been carefully considered and justified by evidence and logic. Second, requiring accountable officials to address each of these interrelated topics provokes consideration and then composition of an appropriate text. Experience with this documentation scheme attests to its effect on the thinking of accountable officials, promoting the use of evidence and logic in the development of proposed budget allocations. Third, requiring program managers to address each of these interrelated topics provides an evidential base for dynamic implementation monitoring, facilitating the comparison of ongoing results against original intentions. Finally, the suggested typology provides a logical sequence for the presentation of budget documentation. A discussion of each topic statement listed in Exhibit 5.1 follows:

> 1) **Rationale.** Every allocation represents a response to a perceived perplexity, defined as an issue, problem, or opportunity, Consequently, as its most critical element, budget documentation should include a diagnosis that provides a rationale, or "raison d'etre," for the proposed budget and the program or project it will fund or finance. This rationale may reference authoritative and accepted standards of service. Although brevity is prized, the diagnosis must suffice to identify the key variables to be programmatically attacked. In those cases where relevant facts, observations, studies, reports, etc., shed light on the issues, problems and opportunities under consideration, but are too voluminous to include, they can be incorporated by reference, properly sourced as to availability with footnotes. *The identification of key variables and causal relationships is the most important duty of program officials seeking budget allocations.*

2) Goal(s). Goal statements logically follow and relate to the diagnosis. Statements which do not incorporate measurable, time-bound and practical objectives are to be regarded as deficient. These statements provide the essential foundation for work plans and the subsequent periodic performance reviews. Exhibit 5.2 provides guidance on the sentence structure of goal statements.

3) Collaborators/Affected Parties. Serves to identify a) the "upstream" and "downstream" units expected to provide assistance to, or receive assistance from, the units financed by the allocation in question, and b) the population to be served and/or regulated by the activities to be financed by the proposed budget. If sufficiently specific, this description provides a basis for calculating benefits conferred by the proposed budget.

4) Conditions of Performance. Related to the description of collaborators and affected parties, this statement documents the leading ideas, the causal relationships, the assumptions and the standards which influence the size, shape and direction of the proposed activities. Causal relationships, or correlations ($y = f x$) deserve emphasis because they provide budgets with their firmest foundation. The impact (positive or negative) of the proposed resource mix and production techniques on performance ratios should be noted. It takes coordinated, competently executed efforts to produce goal attainment. In formulating proposed budgets, administrators must consider and document the practical aspects of implementation, that is, the internal and external conditions which will make performance possible, including institutional aspects (organization, staffing, staff capability, regulations, procedures, equipment, etc).

V. FORMULATION and DOCUMENTATION GUIDELINES

5) Work Plan. Incorporated by reference in budget documentation, work plans represent the substructure of proposed allocations. At the formulation stage, they should be sufficiently detailed to assure thoughtful consideration of the means of implementation. Work plans list specific activities, the work hours assigned to these activities, and the associated performance indicators (targets), if available. The work hours and performance targets are allocated to time periods to provide benchmarks (milestones) for subsequent performance reviews. Program officials should stand ready to reference and interpret work plans, pointing up relationships to stated problems and goals.

6) Budget. As they display the resource implications of proposed work plans, budget proposal formats should incorporate a funding or financing plan, balanced to the proposed expenditure. The suggested format should also incorporate a concise interpretative commentary relating the proposed allocation to a display of performance data It facilitates the budget process if the format of budget proposals is consistent with that employed in the budget submitted to the Appropriation Authority.

7) Alternatives. By requiring a concise description of alternatives which were considered, but set aside in favor of the preferred solution, this statement encourages program officials to examine options, especially production techniques and resource mixes which might reduce unit costs or improve output per work hour. This statement also gives reviewing officials an opportunity to examine a proposed allocation, and its production arrangements, within a context of approaches and, perhaps, values, other than those recommended by the requester. In those jurisdictions coping with binding budget limitations, program officials may be required to provide prioritized alternatives.

In addition to increasing the probability that proposed allocations are well considered and anchored to specified relationships between intentions and results, the suggested seven-statement topology:

- Provides a logical scheme guiding budgetary thinking. The topical sequence is effective in centering thought on the ways and means of implementation, starting with setting goals and ending with the formulation of work plans.

- Encourages an iterative thought process. The sequence suggests that accountable officials should address the topics, one after the other in the listed order. However, experience indicates that the inter-relatedness of the topics encourages budget formulators to "go back and forth" among them, adding and amending as they develop the text of each. In this connection, the phrase, "the devil is in the details," points up the usefulness of shifting from the general to the particular, and then back again. By alternating levels of abstraction, this iterative process stirs the mind, sparking ideas, clues, cues, insights, scenarios, etc.

- Provides a logical scheme for the composition and presentation of an appropriate interpretative text. As the text is open to choices concerning the level of abstraction, numeric displays can be inserted in text to provide selected levels

V. FORMULATION and DOCUMENTATION GUIDELINES

of detail in support of general propositions. As a rule, no numeric display should be inserted in a text without interpretation.

- Provides a base of evidence and logic to support dynamic implementation monitoring, facilitating the comparison of accumulating results against original intentions.

Experience with this documentation scheme attests to its salubrious effect on the quality of budget documentation, promoting the use of evidence and logic in the development of proposed budget allocations. Requiring such documentation provides a strong basis for performance articulation and usage throughout the budget cycle. As indicated above, an iterative process of shifting between defining problems, setting goal(s), identifying collaborators and affected parties, specifying conditions of performance, and composing work plan(s) and budgets details promotes critical thinking.

Exhibit 5.2   Goal Statement Sentence Structure

	SENTENCE ELEMENT	LANGUAGE ALTERNATIVES
TIME	Dependent Clause	After _____, During _____, By _____,
RESPONSIBILITY	Subject	the _____ team the _____ unit the _____ staff etc.
COMMITMENT	Verb	will...plans...aims...intends, etc.
IMPACT	Verbal Phrase	to increase, to improve... reduce...produce...conduct, etc.
GOAL	Complement, Object	Insert language specifying the goal in measurable terms, e.g., "from an estimated 90% in the current year to 95% next year."

Statements Five and Six, Work Plan and Budget, put "managerial and financial muscle" behind the preferred solution(s) to the perplexity(ies) outlined by Statement One, Program Rationale. The seventh topic, Rejected Alternatives, documents consideration given to alternatives and, most critically, the reasons for their rejection in favor of the preferred solution. The requirement to describe alternatives considered, but rejected, provides appropriations authorities with assurance that the proposed solution satisfies disclosed decision criteria. It also alerts accountable officials to alternatives which might merit exploration for inclusion in future budgets.

In best practice, during the budget formulation period, budget officers should provide consulting service to program officials, focused on proposal formulation and documentation. Of course, to protect the integrity of the process, they must confine their advice to form, rather than substance. For example, it is entirely permissible for budget officers to spark the thinking of program officials by encouraging them to consider irregular, unspecific questions. In this regard, the hypothetical question, *"What if...?"* is particularly useful. Examples: What may happen to performance if this proposed budget is reduced by 10%? What may happen if the mix of resources is changed? Or production techniques?

Presented with expenditure interpretations so documented, how should budget officers respond? This question tracks to the heart of their job philosophy. Of course, they must examine expenditures, per se. However, proposed budgets so carefully crafted, deserve respect and should not be adjusted by the arbitrary cutting of line-item allocations, salaries, supplies, contracts, etc. Consequently, adjustments in program should precede and accompany adjustments in expenditure.

As explored in Part Seven, *Key Task: Assessing the Merit of Allocations*, when presented with well-considered programmatic documentation, budget officers should critically evaluate problem and goal statements, for these provide the expenditure rationale. If satisfied, budget officers can then critically evaluate the five associated statements describing the ways and means of problem solution and goal

V. FORMULATION and DOCUMENTATION GUIDELINES

attainment. To think critically about subject at hand, budget officers require a documentary base facilitating a judgment about the intrinsic merit of a proposed program and its budgetary support. Such a base permits testing a proposed program and budget for effectiveness, efficiency and economy and other measures, such as capital/labor ratios and investment returns.

It is obvious that documentation formulated along the lines suggested above will influence the format and content of supporting programmatic records and procedures, as well as, most crucially, the quality of budgetary thought. Indeed, the recommended statements are designed to increase the probability that that proposed budgets are well-thought out. In my experience, requiring program officials to so document their proposals causes them to rationalize their proposals, dropping some aspects as indefensible and changing others to comply with the desired tendency of the measurements subsumed by values of the efficacy triad.

Also, consider this: Given the deadline pressures on budget officers during the budget formulation period, budget officers must ration their time. In any given year, budget officers can only target selected programs and budgets for in-depth evaluation. Requiring budget proposers to meet high standards of documentation helps to ensure that all programs and budgets are carefully formulated, even though only a selected number may be subject to in-depth analysis in any given year.

Obviously, time constraints have implications for work commitments prior to the annual call for estimates. As noted in Part One, budget officers must be prepared to teach budget-related skills to budgetary participants. Experience with the documentation requirements listed in Exhibit 5.1 indicates that many program officials have trouble defining program rationale and specifying goals, as paradoxical as that may seem.

(An author's aside: I have frequently encountered officials whose conceptions of programmatic problems fail to specify the critical/causal variables to be addressed, or who cannot identify quantified, time-bound, practical program goals.)

Budgetary Thought for Budget Officers

Budget officers cannot assume that budget requesters understand the required documentation standards, or that all possess requisite knowledge and skill. If they are of any size, governments of general jurisdiction will employ a certain number of program officials with budgeting duties who need specific training in budget formulation practice and procedures, as well as instruction in the ways and means of performance improvement. Because statements of issues, problems and opportunities provide the "raison d'etre," or rationale for budgets, and the activity they will fund, the specification of critical and/or causal variables and causal relationships is a most important budget formulation task. Goal specification then logically follows. . Most assuredly, a recommended budget formulation training program may include other subjects, depending on an analysis of training needs, but concerns about the quality of statements concerning program rationale and goals are paramount. Although brevity is prized, the diagnosis must be sufficiently broad and deep to identify the key variables which may be made subject to programmatic activity. Consider the following statement concerning motor vehicle conditions related to accidents:

> In the _____ fiscal year, _____ vehicles, __% of total registered vehicles, were subject to safety inspections. Of these, _____, or __ %, were found unroadworthy. In that same fiscal year, vehicle safety deficiencies figured in _____ accidents, or __ % of the total.

In addition to identifying "vehicle safety deficiencies" as a key variable, the statement identifies a possible causal relationship between the key variable and an undesirable outcome, (accidents) even though the relationship, itself, is not mathematically specified. This points the way to a discussion of programmatic action (increased inspections) which might decisively alter the problem situation in desired ways.

Statements concerning program rationale should include an interpretation of current year performance, measured against established

V. FORMULATION and DOCUMENTATION GUIDELINES

targets. That discussion provides an indispensable platform for the development of the proposed work plan and budget for the upcoming year. At this point, it is necessary to point out that mission statements are no substitute for statements citing program rationale. As mission statements assume programmatic solutions, rather than define issues, problems and opportunities, such statements are best formulated and expressed in the context of goal statements and work plans.

As disinterested persons working at the intersection of finance and programmatic interests, budget officers are uniquely placed, and, if schooled for the purpose, qualified to teach the ways and means of performance improvement. Whether working alone, or in concert with others in the larger jurisdictions, budget officers should visualize themselves as the faculty of an informal administrative academy.

Encouraging and Applying Critical Thought

Unquestionably, critical thinking" is the most important mental instrument of budget officers — and the greatest intellectual need in politics and government! By precept and example, budget officers should encourage the application of critical thinking throughout their jurisdiction. Critical thinking comes into play when people are in doubt and/or face choices between inaction and courses of action. As conflict is endemic in political environments, perplexities abound. Doubt about what to do causes officials to frame their perplexity in problematic terms. Perplexity fosters learning and creates opportunities to consider change in external conditions and alternative courses of action. When perplexities rise to the stage of practical politics, they may be distinguished as "issues" rather than "problems." Issues are resolved, settled by negotiation, bargaining and compromise, but, if not, by imposition or neglect. Problems are solved by reasoning. Although many will find it too fine, the distinction between issues and problems is significant. The political arts of negotiation, bargaining and compromise are not appropriate modes of behavior for budget officers. Budget officers are most effective when their talent is applied to solving problems, especially in those cases when issues can be converted into problems that yield to critical thought.

Although the budget formulation training syllabus will vary by jurisdiction, based on perceived knowledge and skill deficiencies, no jurisdiction can go far wrong by teaching its staff to employ mathematical modeling as a technique of programming and budgeting. The practice of mathematical modeling has many valuable "side-effects," including, most importantly, inescapable requirements for critical thinking. As the accountable officials, budget officers should strive to foster the use of mathematical modeling in budget formulation. Budget officers must master the technique and be capable of assisting program officials in its use. Most crucially, they must respect and support initiatives advanced by program officials based on correlations. With the advance of computer technology, it is becoming easier to add multiple identifiers to a jurisdiction's chart of accounts, exploit the utilities of management accounting and "model" an expenditure pattern. Applying mathematical thinking to the task of assessing the merit of proposed allocations is considered at some length in Part Seven.

As commonly practiced, proposed budgets are built up, item by item, program-by-program. To be sure, this process of aggregation produces certain benefits, such as, responsible (but not necessarily accurate) estimates, extensive documentation, orderly reviews, etc. The process has, however, a major drawback: It tends to immerse budget participants in detail ("drown" is perhaps a better word), making it hard to get and keep a "sense-of-the-whole." Broad perspectives are very important in budget work. Indeed, public officials, including budget officers, who cannot maintain an adequate conception of overall mission and effectiveness are forced to specialize in trivia, suffering impaired judgment and reduced relevance in the bargain. As all budget officers know, it is not easy to rise above the flood of minutia. This is the virtue of "modeling" procedures. In order to model, accountable officials must first slice through masses of fact and value to isolate those few key

V. FORMULATION and DOCUMENTATION GUIDELINES

variables which "make a difference" in performance, that is, control the ability of applied resources to achieve desired goal(s). If they can then specify the relationship of these key variables to one another, and to the goal(s), they will be in position to construct and use models in the budgetary process.

Best described as hypothetical statements, models involve an ordered set of assumptions about causes, effects, and objectives. Models can be very elaborate, but not necessarily so. Variables abound! The search for variables can put a variety of viewpoints to work. Indeed, modeling offers opportunities for constructive participation by "collaborators and affected parties" identified in Statement Three of the suggested budget formulation and documentation topology (See Exhibit 5.1.) Allocation proposals developed according to the specifications listed in Exhibit 5.1, help to identify likely independent and dependent variables that can be used to build models. The search for variables should also include reviews of technical and critical literature related to the subject matter in question.

By exploiting existing data sources, or by organizing special data arrays, officials can employ correlation studies to assess the weight of each independent variable. If a selected variable is found to be sufficiently influential, the budgetary implications are obvious. On the other hand, should any independent variable prove to have little or no relationship to the dependent variable (the objective), other variables may be substituted in the equation, and tested for significance,

It is one of the great advantages of modeling that, once equations have been established, a model builder can play with a number of likely variables, searching for that combination of variables which reduces the amount of "unexplained" variation to a minimum. While not minimizing the computational problems involved in modeling of the type discussed above, it is fair to say that problems of data availability and validity will prove the most vexing. Measurement problems should not cause us to turn away from significant variables. After all, if we give up because of measurement difficulties, we will not be able to model at all, as many of the most significant variables in public services are difficult to measure.

Summing up, the abstract nature of models centers attention on important and effective variables, to the exclusion of all else. Their use especially benefits budget officers, who are frequently distracted by peripheral issues and administrative trivia. Additionally, modeling practices treat budgets as rather continuous experiments, undermining the inertial power of established practice. Models belong in every jurisdiction's budget toolbox. Definitely, budget officers should strive to cause them to be built and used!

Macro-Micro Reconciliation

Many jurisdictions are subject to tax and expenditure limitations, or have voluntarily adopted a "top-down" approach to budget formulation, based on adoption of budget constraints. Whether coping with an amount of allowable deficit, or maximum expenditure and revenue amounts, striving to attain fixed fiscal targets will definitely affect the budget amount – that is, after all, the purpose of budget constraints.

With regard to budget formulation procedures, however, the leading executive officials can respond to the imposition of limits on their discretion in three basic ways. First, they can permit program officials to make recommendations without reference to limitations, a basic feature of the executive budget model. They trust that they are, assisted by budget officers, capable of adjusting allocation requests to satisfy the required constraint. On other hand, the leading executive officials may choose to shift the burden of choice to program officials, adopting a strategy of "prior restraint." They use some sort of formula to set limits on the freedom of program officials to formulate expenditure proposals, for example: limit proposed budgets to current year revised estimates, reduce all budgets by 10%, no new positions, etc. (It is instructive to note that when jurisdictions are faced with the necessity to reduce budgets, their leaders often cut expenditures arbitrarily, leaving the task of

V. FORMULATION and DOCUMENTATION GUIDELINES

program adjustment to program officials.) Finally, the leading executive officials can involve program officials in the compliance process by requiring them to prioritize incremental and decremental alternatives to a base amount, such as, the current year revised estimate. This methodology captures the best thinking of program officials and provides the leading executive officials with an options menu, a mix of choices that includes consideration of desirable program investments.

Exhibit 5.3 An Indicative Example of an Options Worksheet

	COST CENTER "A"	COST CENTER "B"	COST CENTER "N"	TOTAL
Total Prioritized Increases	1200	2400		
Etc.				
Proposed Increment - Priority 3	40	80		
Proposed Increment - Priority 2	60	120		
Proposed Increment - Priority 1	100	200		
Current Year Revised Estimate	1000	2000		
Proposed Decrement - Priority 1	(100)	(200)		
Proposed Decrement - Priority 2	(60)	(120)		
Proposed Decrement - Priority 3	(40)	(80)		
Etc.				
Total Prioritized Decreases	800	1600		

Exhibit 5.3 displays a sample worksheet listing alternatives offered by program officials. The sample worksheet is keyed to an estimate of current year revised expenditures. It lists potential increases and decreases related to current estimated expenditure. Submitted by all program agencies, the information so assembled can be used to adjust proposed allocations to meet fiscal policy targets – an inherently difficult task. Requiring agencies to submit incremental and

decremental priorities provides an organized data base for the consideration of policy options. With indicative entries, this sample worksheet displays programmatic options within specified expenditure limits, in this case, up 20% and down 20% from the current year revised estimate. Aggregating priorities across all agencies (decremental Priority 1, for example), provides total amounts useful in adjusting proposed budgets to a given fiscal policy target.

Program officials can be required to contribute directly to a jurisdiction-wide prioritization process. Unquestionably, by their position and knowledge, program officials are most competent to prioritize proposals for funding. Obtaining priority designations from program officials can be made a purpose of Statement Six, *Alternatives*, listed in Exhibit 5.1, *Formulation and Documentation Guidelines.* Statement Six can be used to institutionalize an approach to prioritization which reduces the need for arbitrary action by executive and legislative leaders by giving due weight to recommendations of program officials.

Some additional thoughts on the assessment problem before concluding this commentary on budget formulation and documentation:

Addressing the Assessment Problem

The primary purpose of the recommended documentation requirements is clear and laudable: Proposals to spend public funds should be thoroughly thought out by their advocates. Cogent justifications for proposals to "spend other people's money" should be available for critical review and possible amendment or rejection, prior to adoption by appropriation authorities. Ironically, however, any process that produces efficacious programs and cogent budget proposals, based thereon, complicates the allocation process at levels of decision where proposals become competitive — and must be measured against one anther and limited resources. On this point, a remark once made by a legislator may be regarded as quintessential: "I dislike performance budgets because they provide information that makes cutting more difficult."

V. FORMULATION and DOCUMENTATION GUIDELINES

The frequently noted resistance and/or indifference of legislators to results-oriented budgeting can be traced to worries that budgets cast in programmatic terms foster conflict, rather than compromise, by focusing attention on the ends of government activity rather than the means, that is, expenditure, per se. This point of view was advanced by Aaron Wildavsky in his influential book, *The Politics of the Budgetary Process* (1964). Expressed concerns about possible consequences of enhancing the quality of budget proposals must be taken seriously. They direct our attention to the perplexities facing the officials who must assess the intrinsic and relative merit of proposed allocations.

Obviously, the recommended requirements are designed to encourage the formulation and documentation of soundly-based proposals to "spend other people's money" — even at the cost of increasing the discomfort of the officials who must decide among well-supported competitive proposals. But, it is equally obvious that proposals justified by the recommended data arrays and interpretative text also provide reviewing officials with decision-related information, should they have the wit and will to apply it to the assessment task. As a case in point, consider the intent of Statement Seven, *Alternatives*. This requirement fosters flexible thinking and a search for options by requiring program officials to examine and document alternatives to their preferred course of action. Flexibility and choice are prized values in the public budgeting process, which tends to favor "what is" over "what could be." Specifically, Statement Seven encourages reviewing officials, especially budget officers, to search for situations marked by declining marginal productivity, that is, situations where divestments and transfers based on divestment can produce significant gains in effectiveness, efficiency and economy.

Taken as a whole, the documentation provided by the seven interrelated statements encourages and enables reviewing officials to apply objective, rather than subjective, standards of judgment. Indeed, well-conceived and documented proposals are a condition precedent for effective application of the analytical approaches recommended by Part

Seven, which is devoted to the ways and means of assessing the intrinsic and relative merit of competitive allocation proposals. Whatever one may say to chief executives and legislators about the significance of programmatic data, the value of well-documented proposals to budget officers can not be overstated.

VI. PRELIMINARY WORK

Perhaps no other aspect of budgetary practice embraces as much variety as the work undertaken by governments of general jurisdiction in anticipation of an upcoming budget. Lacking a common conception of best practice, the following discussion of exemplary budget planning rests on the organizational and procedural assumptions of the "executive budgeting" model. Consequently, it is assumed that, as the new fiscal period approaches, budget officers engage in various forms of budget planning, if only to update forms and instructions issued to facilitate the budget formulation process for the upcoming fiscal period. Also, in well ordered jurisdictions, its finance establishment participates in the formulation of the upcoming budget by calculating pro forma estimates of current year revenue and expenditure flows, and year-end fund balances. Most assuredly, anticipating the call for expenditure estimates, program officials throughout the jurisdiction formulate budget proposals. Structured or unstructured, the months approaching a new fiscal period are a time of excitement and fermentation.

Recognizing the importance and potentialities of the anticipatory period, and consistent with our theme that appropriate procedures serve to stimulate and channel budgetary thinking in desired directions, we will dwell on intellectual requirements, and the associated institutionalized processes which can nourish the minds of all officials participating in the anticipatory budgetary process. As recommended herein, these and other forms of anticipatory thinking and action can (and should) be integrated into a cohesive, jurisdiction-wide process. The timing and key elements of this organized anticipatory process are listed in Exhibit 6.1, *Budget Cycle Components*.

Exhibit 6.1 Budget Cycle Components

ANTICIPATORY PROCESS						
ASSESSMENT	PROPOSALS	BUDGETING	IMPLEMENTATION			
Current Fiscal Year, Months 6-8		Last 4 Months	Quarter 1	2	3	4
Survey of Issues, Problems and Opportunities. Selection of Initiatives. Statement of Financial Capability.	COMPOSITION - Resource Mobilization Methodology - Fiscal & Budgetary Perspective - Budget Call	FORMULATION 1) Rationale 2) Goal Statement 3) Collaborators & Affected Parties 4) Conditions of Performance 5) Work Plan 6) Budget 7) Alternatives ADOPTION				
			- Work Plan - Allotment - Performance Review - Corrective Action	" " " "	" " " 	" " " "
			ANTICIPATORY PROCESS, Months 6-8			

    The anticipatory process should produce three valuable documents, 1) a revenue mobilization methodology, 2) a financial capability statement, and 3) a fiscal and budgetary perspective, the latter resting on the key findings and recommendations of the first two.

    As recommended, this process gives programmatic and centralized process agency officials an organized opportunity to work together with "tools" readily at hand, but not always "working hand-in-hand." This anticipatory effort culminates with the formulation of a Fiscal and Budgetary Perspective. In turn, this "outlook" document serves as the essential reference for the composition of the chief executive's Call for Estimates, initiating the formulation of detailed budget proposals. To be conducted effectively, a jurisdiction-wide anticipatory process requires a

VI. PRELIMINARY WORK

sharply focused, vigorously managed research program, best conducted by a broad-based team appointed by its chief executive. Arrangements should include administrative support drawn from the jurisdiction's finance establishment, including, most crucially, financial and budget officers, who, by function and knowledge, are appropriate officials to organize and support the process. The day-to-day management of the research process should be assigned to budget officers familiar with the subjects on the research agenda. Budget officers should also be responsible for the production and distribution of the Fiscal and Budgetary Perspective and the subsequent Call for Estimates.

Planning officials have an important role in an anticipatory process. Typically, the larger governments of general jurisdiction have planning agencies. Where established and professionally staffed, the contribution of planning agencies significantly influences official thinking about the future. Obviously, planning agency data, analyses and recommendations should strongly condition the formulation of fiscal and budgetary perspectives. Of course, this injunction assumes the existence of a harmonious, respectful relationship between the finance establishment and the planning agency. Reportedly, however, many finance officials are rather wary of planning agency thinking and activity, and vice versa. Mutual suspicion is usually rooted in an environment of competition and conflict. The reasons for mutual worries are understandable, given the fact that, inevitably, planning agency thinking has finance and budgetary implications, the thrust of which may not be appreciated by finance officials.

Consider the following typical circumstances: Usually, planning agencies play a dominant role in the composition of government capital investment plans. Moreover, in many jurisdictions, planning agencies establish and maintain key relationships with donor agencies, including the multi-lateral financial institutions. If so, this connection provides planning agencies with a formidable power base. Further, planning agencies with responsibility for economic analysis are usually responsible for defining the relationship of prospective budgets to prospective estimates of Gross Domestic Product. This work usually results in a recommended "budget constraint." Representing a key variable in the determination of fiscal policy, the recommended constraint usually gets serious consideration during the formulation of prospective budgets.

Given the range and the financial import of these planning activities, it is not surprising that many finance officials are wary of planning agencies. On the other hand, planning officials may not eagerly seek and maintain consultative relationships with finance officials, who they may view as representing an institutionalized "No!" (It must be admitted, however, that "program-oriented" finance officials are relatively rare.) Planning officials may regard the result of such consultations as "prior restraint," that is, pressure impinging on independent staff thinking and objectivity. This type of situation can be exacerbated when finance and planning officials pursue their work in relative isolation from one another. If so, they are more likely to be surprised and upset when recommendations surface during the anticipatory phase of the budget cycle. Regarding this prospect, knowledgeable observers have noted that competition and conflict are inherent factors in the finance-planning relationship, but, with disclosure and transparency, can produce better-considered decisions. Dynamic implementation monitoring, as herein recommended, provides a handy institutional vehicle for enhancing disclosure and transparency across organizational lines. A dynamic monitoring process can be structured so that finance establishment and planning agency staffs participate in each other's periodic, formal performance reviews. Knowing about each other's activity during the fiscal year may help reduce tension between the staffs of these two important governmental units. The concept of dynamic monitoring is discussed in some detail later on.

Strictly speaking, the future is unknown, and, unknowable. Yet, pragmatically, we all continuously count on regular recurrences, *ceteris paribus*. This tacit assumption of regularity has profound effects, for our sense of it emboldens us to anticipate and to plan. It has been wisely said that the assumption of regularity gives us the nerve to anticipate and plan, and most important, to act! As a case in point, budget adoption represents a legislative act of faith that desired programmatic values can be realized at a future time. This faith is usually braced by a predictable application of administrative and accounting controls. Further, although a budget may be regarded as a plan, unforeseen contingencies inevitably require its adjustment during the implementation period.

Legislative adoption of estimated revenues is also an act of faith, modified by an awareness that considerable variation in amounts eventually collected is a strong probability. Clearly, given the importance of attaining revenue targets, governments are well advised to invest in proven ways and means of revenue mobilization, as will be recommended, to maximize collections in the face of inevitable revenue contingencies.

In sum, although plans are manifestly fallible, conceived in terms of design and control, government leaders are well advised to engage in anticipatory exercises, thus institutionalizing leadership thinking about the fiscal future. Due to the intrinsic unreliability of prediction, a weak, haphazard approach to anticipating future events will surely waste time and resources, and, quite probably will have regrettable consequences.

EXHIBIT 6.2 Characteristics of Government Capability

ORIENTATION	CHARACTERISTICS	CAPABILITY
NEGATIVE	Behavior: Inactive Policy: Subordination Philosophy: Fatalism	Power to establish desired future states forsaken.
NEUTRAL	Behavior: Reactive Policy: Adjustment Philosophy: Stoicism	Power to establish desired future states circumstantial.
POSITIVE	Behavior: Active Policy: Leadership Philosophy: Dynamism	Power to establish desired future states nurtured and exerted.

The terms, Negative, Neutral and Positive, are generalizations, representing the characteristic, or predominant, disposition of government leaders toward their responsibility for actions deliberately shaping the physical, social and economic environment of their jurisdictions.

Governments are key institutions for selecting and attaining desired community goals. However, governments vary in their capability to fulfill this expectation. Exhibit 6.2, *Characteristics of Government Capability*, identifies three categories of government capability, listing key defining characteristics of each. A brief commentary on each orientation follows:

> Negative Orientation. At the negative pole of this capability spectrum, one places those governments which pursue minimum service and regulatory policies, their leaders taking a rather fatalistic position on social and economic situations. The officials of governments of this type are not likely to support investments in the development of fiscal and budget perspectives.
>
> Neutral Orientation. Those governments which usually strive to attain and maintain themselves in a harmonious balance with social and economic formations and forces may also, circumstances permitting, strive to establish desired future states and situations. Should governments of this type adopt formal fiscal and budget perspectives, they will find that their ability to take advantage of opportunities, as they arise, will be significantly enhanced. Indeed, they may find that the introduction of formal fiscal and budgetary perspectives produces a significant change in the fundamental relationship between the government and its citizens, with citizens expecting a stronger, more efficient and effective management of services and regulations.
>
> Positive Orientation. Governments which formulate multi-year capital investment programs have already introduced processes consistent with the logic of trying

VI. PRELIMINARY WORK

to anticipate and control the future. The same may be said for governments which develop and implement land use plans, zoning and multi-year operating budgets. Officials of governments which already try to exert positive leadership in defining and realizing community goals will find that the formulation of fiscal and budgetary perspectives provides a comprehensive core process enhancing the efficiency and effectiveness of all its policy and management tools, especially budget formulation and implementation.

As my experience accumulated over the years, I came to favor the term, "perspective," rather than "plan" to identify the product of the anticipatory process herein recommended. The term, plan (often coupled with "strategic"), suggests a narrowing of options, a series of precise steps and the specification of the "one best way" — characteristics which tend to vex political minds which crave options and prize discretion. In contrast, a "perspective" suggests a point of view, a presentation of related facts, opinions and possible happenings, displayed in a context of appropriate depth and latitude.

Exhibit 6.3 Elements of an Anticipatory Process

1.0 ORGANIZATIONAL REQUIREMENTS

    A. Adopt a research agenda, initiating the budget cycle.
    B. Organize, specifying the role and responsibilities of staff assigned to research teams, with budget officers serving as their secretariat.
    C. Communicate and Document, stressing consultation, clearance, disclosure and transparency.
    D. Control the research process, via dynamic monitoring.

2.0 PROCESS

    2.1 Survey Issues, Problems and Opportunities
        A. Conduct Public Forums
        B. Convene Technical Conferences
        C. Commission Technical Papers

    2.2 Formulate and Document Financial Capability
        A. Estimate resources and formulate a Mobilization Methodology
        B. Formulate a Multi-year Financial Capability Statement

    2.3 Formulate and Document Proposed Initiatives
        A. Select key issues, problems and opportunities
        B. Formulate proposed initiatives:*
            1) Define program rationale
            2) State goal(s) in a multi-year perspective
            3) Identify collaborators and affected parties
            4) Identify conditions required for goal attainment
            5) Formulate preferred solution(s) and tentative multi-year budget
            6) Identify alternatives considered, but rejected, and rejection rationale

    2.4 Complete and Submit Fiscal & Budgetary Perspective

* Descriptions of proposed initiatives need only be detailed to the extent required to establish them as candidates for consideration in the upcoming budget.

VI. PRELIMINARY WORK

Organizational requirements and a suggested agenda for the formulation of perspectives are outlined in Exhibit 6.3, *Elements of an Anticipatory Process*. Perspectives confer the following advantages:

1) The formulation of fiscal and budgetary perspectives, as recommended, tends to promote organizational cohesion by improving inter-agency communication.

2) The educational impacts of well-executed perspectives on officials and other interested and affected parties can be significant, and, indeed, this potential effect provides perspectives with sufficient rationale.

However, the strongest rationale for establishing an anticipatory organization and process, as outlined by Exhibit 6.3, lies in its stimulation of decision-related research, conducted outside normal budget and law-making channels. The dearth of decision-related research on public problems is a grave weakness of contemporary governance, world-wide. As the tide of science-based technological innovation sweeps onward, governments find themselves enmeshed in internal and external complexities which simultaneously demand new policy decisions, yet obscure potential consequences. These complexities confront policy-making officials with challenges to their knowledge, their experience and their will to act. In the web of interactions defining the complexity of modern life, public issues, problems and opportunities are increasingly difficult to properly define, let alone satisfactorily addressed by government initiatives.

Significantly, the spread of wireless and internet-based communication has increased the volume of transmissions and information about public affairs, without noticeably enhancing the effectiveness of public decision-making processes. If anything, the increase in the total flow of fact and opinion tends to produce a daily plebiscite on what is "true" and "good," undermining the role of analysis, synthesis and deliberation in shaping public policy. The anticipatory process outlined by Exhibit 6.3 has features which institutionalize systematic discussion and reflection on complex matters by qualified parties. As noted, the process of developing perspectives begins with an assessment of issues, problems and opportunities, conducted by means of public forums, technical conferences and technical papers – a process designed to encourage the vigorous participation of non-politicized, non-bureaucratized parties. This helps to counterbalance the policy biases of legislators, administrators, and the influence of special pleaders who work tirelessly for their client's interest in the political background.

As recommended herein, fiscal and budgetary perspectives reflect the results of organized thinking about the efficacy of present and possible future policies and programs.

Exhibit 6.4 Modalities of Projection

	PURPOSE	ACTION	CONSEQUENCE ?
1	Identify future consequences of current policies, programs and projects.	Continue without change	Then, the following may happen: Projected Consequence #1 Projected Consequence #2 Etc.
2	Identify changes in current programmatic activity which might bring about a desired future state.	Introduce now	Then, the following may happen: Projected Consequence #1 Projected Consequence #2 Etc.
3	Identify future policy and programmatic initiatives which might bring about a desired future state. .	Introduce later	Then, the following may happen: Projected Consequence #1 Projected Consequence #2 Etc.

At this point, consult Exhibit 6.4, *Modalities of Projection*. As outlined, thinking about the future takes three forms. The first two modes of thinking about the future assess the future consequences of current action, or inaction. The third mode centers attention on the future

VI. PRELIMINARY WORK

consequences of future action, the most popular conception of planning, that is, doing something in the future to affect the future. Officials who participate in the development of annual fiscal and budgetary perspectives will undoubtedly find themselves engaged in all three modalities of thought. The topology displayed in Exhibit 6.4 provides a format for process controls, useful in monitoring the status of work on each problem, issue or opportunity brought under consideration during the development of the fiscal and budgetary perspective.

An anticipatory process is a complex undertaking. Consequently, when making organizational and procedural arrangements, the accountable officials are advised to recognize and respect this complexity. If not, the process will be ineffectively conducted and poorly related to key policy and management processes. Respecting this complexity, the accountable officials should consider the following factors:

> *First*, the process requires the cooperation of many parties, willing and unwilling, within and without government. (Many career-conscious officials regard assessments and projections, if at all possible, as risky business, best avoided.) To adequately define issues, problems and opportunities, and to formulate likely programmatic aand project solutions requires a strong institutional commitment to research, consultation with affected parties and inter-agency collaboration. Minimally, the research agenda should include a) public forums, b) technical conferences, and c) technical papers. *Moreover*, the research requires valid, relevant data, and dedicated researchers, impossible to obtain and maintain without clear and steady institutional commitments. *Furthermore*, as the implementation of recommend initiatives will require legislative support, organizational arrangements should include reporting commitments and the constructive involvement of policy leaders. *Finally*, the timely

development of perspectives requires management attention and persistence, best expressed through dynamic monitoring of the research process.

The production of recommended fiscal and budgetary perspectives, referencing the findings and recommendations of reports concerning revenue mobilization and a financial capability, provides a foundation for the composition and issuance of a "call for estimates." The anticipatory process should be completed no later than the end of the eighth month of the current fiscal year. This timetable permits the annual call for estimates, initiating the budget formulation process, to reference the results of the anticipatory effort. It is important to note that, if it has been conducted as recommended, the jurisdiction's program officials have been key participants and contributors to the process. Consequently, no accountable program official should be surprised by the contents of the call for estimates. During the budget formulation process, accountable program officials have an opportunity to consider proposed initiatives in depth, and, if acceptable in concept, refine them as needed for incorporation in their budget requests. Ideally, the concerned program officials are free to modify or reject proposed initiatives. Objection and rejection are always possibilities in an open process designed to elicit and respect facts and thoughtful opinions.

Generally, participants find an anticipatory process stimulating. Easy-sailing visions of future projects and programs ply the mind, even though seasoned officials know that the future, when encountered, is usually a sea laced with rocks and shoals. The officials managing an anticipatory process must counter this tendency by encouraging the assigned staff to apply a "criterion of implementability" to proposed initiatives, strictly referenced to estimates of financial capability. Concentrating on implementable initiatives conserves analytical time and effort and tends to produce better proposal designs.

Fiscal and budgetary perspectives should be critically shaped by resource availability. When competently estimated, a statement of

VI. PRELIMINARY WORK

financial capability effectively limits the scope and, possibly, the direction of the research effort. Researchers who invest precious time and effort in considering proposed programs and projects that, no matter how meritorious, will require resources beyond the boundary of defined financial capability, risk their credibility with officials, and the public, alike. Obviously, to be of maximum utility, statements of financial capability should be composed by finance officials very early in the research process, or, even better, preceding it. In this regard, it is also efficacious to make the budget staff responsible for the organization and conduct of the anticipatory process, and the composition of the Fiscal and Budgetary Perspective. This procedure draws budget officers into program development at formative stages, reducing the chances of arbitrary revisions during budget formulation phase.

The recommended anticipatory process (featuring consultation, disclosure, communication and transparency) provides a necessary, but insufficient, foundation for effective implementation of initiatives, if and when adopted. Effective implementation of project and programmatic initiatives requires the integrated employment of four key instruments: 1) work plans, 2) allotments, 3) dynamic monitoring, that is, periodic "before-the-fact" formal performance reviews, and 4) corrective action when behind schedule. These instruments of implementation also apply to the research program conducted during an anticipatory process. The requirements of "dynamic" implementation are explored in detail in Part Seven.

Generally, even under the best of circumstances, government leaders find program and project implementation beset with difficulties. Indeed, observers familiar with strategic planning efforts frequently mention implementation failures. Instruction on the hazards of implementation is provided by Aaron Wildavsky and Jeffrey Pressman, *Implementation,* (Berkeley: University of California Press, 1973). A case study of the failure of an economic development program in Oakland, California, the authors conclude that the problems of implementation must be an integral consideration during program formulation, not a process that takes place after the adoption of its design. Logically, means and ends should be made partially dependent on each other. Certainly, sound advice.

To repeat, the intrinsic difficulties of government program and project implementation deserve formal recognition and respect by officials managing an anticipatory process. Emphatically, implementation should be the *first and abiding* concern of officials formulating and reviewing program and project proposals. Consequently, before channeling time and effort selecting and formulating proposed programs and projects, the assigned staff must weigh the contingencies of implementation, especially the vital matter of financial support for proposed initiatives. The following practices deserve consideration:

- Involving implementing officials, and interested and affected parties, in the anticipatory process. This is especially important in the initial survey phase.

- Conducting the anticipatory process before the start of the annual budget cycle, requiring the submission of the Fiscal and Budgetary Perspective to the chief executive prior to the call for budget estimates. The initiatives favorably noted in the Call for Estimates obviously have a high probability of adoption, and eventual implementation.

- Requiring the jurisdiction's chief financial officer to provide a multi-year financial capability statement early in the anticipatory process, estimating the resources available to support

VI. PRELIMINARY WORK

initiatives. The concept of available resources embraces 1) estimated changes in revenue collections, 2) uncommitted balances, and 3) borrowing power.

- Employing a selective approach to proposals, applying the criterion of implementability, referenced to the multi-year financial capability statement. This concentration on implementable initiatives conserves analytical time and effort and tends to produce better proposal designs.

- Providing an "executive presence" during the Anticipatory Process by employing budget officers as the secretariat for the assigned research teams, responsible for organization and conduct of the process, and the composition of the resulting reports. This procedure draws budget officers into program development at formative stages, reducing the chances of arbitrary revisions during budget formulation.

One final comment before turning to the vital subject of resource mobilization — an abiding interest of all officials participating in an Anticipatory Process: By organizational logic, the assigned research team should rely on the jurisdiction's financial staff to define financial capability. In this connection, it must be noted that not all program officials are comfortable with the task of formulating expenditure (and revenue) projections, especially if they reach too far forward into an uncertain future. To mitigate this reluctance, the research team must work very closely and cooperatively with accountable finance, planning and program personnel, and, if required, possess sufficient knowledge to assist in the formulation of the essential financial capability statement.

Task 1. Mobilize Resources

The task of developing a methodology for acquiring funding/financing for an upcoming budget should be initiated and completed very early in the Anticipatory Process. As the time for the issuance of the budget call approaches, government leaders must assess the jurisdiction's capability to fund and, if loans are required, finance contemplated expenditures. By observation and report, the quality of this assessment varies significantly from year-to-year among jurisdictions. Apparently, governments invest in systematic revenue research only when inescapable revenue "shortfalls" loom, and even then, tend to limit their exertions to closing the estimated revenue-expenditure gap, or forego such exertions entirely in favor of "deficit spending." Ironically, despite its transcendent importance, many officials seem to regard resource mobilization as a rather pedestrian (even distasteful) process, necessary to be sure, but not attended by the interest and excitement associated with expenditures. Typical points of organizational weakness include:

1) The well-nigh universal failure of governments to require their program officials to pursue revenue potentials with the same intensity they devote to the formulation and advocacy of desired expenditures.

2) Budget officers too preoccupied (fascinated would be a better word) with expenditures to give revenues the attention they deserve.

VI. PRELIMINARY WORK

3) Equally damaging, the failure to require revenue collection officials (who, wary of the viciousness of revenue politics, typically bury themselves in their collection routines) to provide systematic, jurisdiction-wide leadership and technical support for revenue policy and management research.

Resource mobilization procedures are not nearly as rationalized, or consistently applied, as those prescribed for expenditures. Tellingly, the literature concerning resource mobilization procedures is sparse, indeed, compared to the volumes available on expenditures. While far from exhaustive, and necessarily quite general, this brief recital of acknowledged deficiencies in the resource mobilization process serves to introduce and justify the remedies suggested here, principally the adoption of a formal process for the mobilization of resources, using the formulation, adoption and execution of an annual Resource Mobilization Methodology (RMM) as its linchpin. Further, as indicated by the revenue estimates required to complete Financial Capability Statements, the formulation of an annual RMM is a key step in the development of an annual Fiscal and Budgetary Perspective.

Resource mobilization is exacting work. Doing it well requires persistent executive support, continuous coordination, a firm policy and management action plan and, then, relentless monitoring. In contrast to expenditure formulation, which is infused with the interest of motivated officials, the mobilization of budgetary resources requires a more principled management commitment to its institutional underpinnings. These underpinning include (a) clear, unequivocal expressions of executive interest, (b) adoption of research agendas and work plans, (c) formation and supervision of an inter-agency team, and (d) periodic performance reviews.

Budgetary Thought for Budget Officers

If properly institutionalized, as recommended, the resource mobilization process will provide government officials with well-grounded opportunities to 1) foster equity among those required to pay taxes, fees and service charges, and, 2) secure sufficient resources to fund needed and desired programs and investments. These are extremely important public values. To be perceived as fair and effective, governments must actively strive for revenue equity and revenue sufficiency. Governments expressing these important public values 1) promote civic morale and cohesion, and, simultaneously 2) nurture financial support for beneficial programs and projects. Certainly, the maintenance of equitable revenue policies tends to make it easier to secure public support for revenue measures which pay for needed and desired services and investments. In turn, governments which provide quality services tend to find citizens more willing to pay taxes, fees and service charges, making it easier to adopt revenue measures clearly related to valued service benefits. Thus, revenue equity and revenue sufficiency are complementary values, the struggle to attain one assisting in the struggle to attain the other. Conversely, an acknowledged deficiency in striving for either one of these values cannot help but impede the attainment of the other. Officials who strive for revenue equity and sufficiency will find their work facilitated by the annual production and execution of a Resource Mobilization Methodology. The suggested process has an exceptionally strong rationale. It merits institutionalization, and leadership commitment.

Obviously, the revenue situation conditions the size and shape of service programs and public investments. Reciprocally, the size and shape of service programs and investments frequently affect revenue potentials, especially when service costs are partially or fully billed to service beneficiaries. Moreover, the implementation of revenue recommendations, itself, may require resources, and, thus, have budgetary implications. When revenue projections are incorporated in annual funding plans, the supporting policy and management actions become significant monitoring considerations for those officials responsible for

VI. PRELIMINARY WORK

managing the jurisdiction's cash. Certainly, the ever-present disposition to delay the implementation of revenue recommendations (increases in service charge rates, for example), will reduce anticipated available cash, and depending on circumstances, may disrupt expenditure plans.

For these reasons, resource mobilization activities should be closely coordinated with budget formulation and other key management processes, especially accounting, performance monitoring and the management of cash. Clearly, this vital matter deserves the unremitting attention of budget officers well versed in the details of effective and efficient resource mobilization.

Recognizing the complexity of resource mobilization, the following factors merit consideration: The collection of government revenues requires the collaboration of many parties, willing and unwilling, within and without government. Understanding the problem presented by each source of revenue, and achieving a satisfactory procedural solution, requires a strong institutional commitment to (a) thorough research, (b) consultation with interested and affected parties and, (c) close inter-agency collaboration. Moreover, revenue research requires valid, relevant data, and dedicated researchers, impossible to obtain and sustain without clear and steady institutional commitments. Furthermore, as many revenue recommendations will require legislative support, organizational arrangements should include commitments to transparency, disclosure, quality reporting and the constructive involvement of policy leaders. Finally, the timely formulation and implementation of revenue measures require management attention and persistence, best expressed through work plans and formal performance reviews.

RMM formulation and implementation requires the cooperation of all officials who have revenue collection responsibilities, usually a numerous group in governments of any size. To obtain and maintain the required cooperation, the jurisdiction's chief executive must actively support the resource mobilization process. This support includes the following steps: 1) establishing a Resource Mobilization Team, 2) setting its research agenda and timetable, 3) conducting management reviews of recommendations, when in draft form, and 4) conducting public hearings on draft recommendations in concert with legislative leaders. With all significant revenue-related officials participating, the management reviews (Step 3) and public hearings (Step 4) serve to advise all interested and affected parties, including the general citizenry, about emerging revenue measures and projections, and their implications for the jurisdiction's service and development plans. These reviews provide a forum for defining and solving any remaining problems in completing the RMM Report.

In conducting research on specific revenues, the assigned staff will draw on many sources of data. To order this process, a file of basic data on every revenue is required. Minimally, this file should include data on the following topics:

1. Name of Revenue
2. Legal Basis
3. Philosophic Basis (including observations about revenue equity/fairness)
4. Source(s)
5. Rate(s)
6. Collection Performance/Projection
7. Collection Effectiveness
8a. Collection Cost
8b. Service Cost (Useful in setting service charges)
9. Collection Efficiency

Additionally, from time to time, pertinent information bearing on resources (reports, articles, etc.) will come to the attention of the RMM Team. This information, properly sourced, dated and filed, should also be readily available. If regular accounting reports do not provide the data required for relating collection and service costs to revenues (data

VI. PRELIMINARY WORK

elements 8a and 8b listed above), the RMM Team must press for the maintenance of records which permit costs, direct and indirect, to be identified and assigned to revenues. Additionally, when they can be clearly associated with the collection of specific revenues, work hours should be so recorded.

Efficacious revenue research must be systematic. A systematic approach requires that a RMM Team, and its assigned staff, assemble data and knowledgeable opinions about various factors likely to affect the amounts collected at various times in the future. The required information must be diligently sought from appropriate agencies, public and private, and carefully documented for inclusion in the RMM files. When used in making projections, sources should be duly noted, and dated. The following checklist can help to ensure that assigned researchers consider key factors conditioning revenue estimates:

1) **Base Estimate.** Each year's projected revenue rests on a base amount. For the upcoming year, the RMM Team should use the latest collection estimate for the current year. For each ensuing year of the multi-year projection, the Team is advised to carry forward the projection established for the previous year.

2) **Coverage.** This factor refers to the effect of action plans to expand the effective coverage of revenue collections, that is, bring the actual collections of a revenue closer to the potential of that revenue. The three topics listed below encourage deep thinking on this critical aspect of revenue management:

   A) **Subjects and Objects.** In its consideration of coverage, the RMM Team should establish a reasonable estimate of the number of objects and/or subjects covered by the taxes, fees and service charges, then compare these estimates with current experience. If a "gap" is identified, the Team should formulate management plans to increase compliance.

B) **Remittances**. In its study of potential, the Team must consider the possibility of "leakage," such as, a business operator keeping a portion of the sales tax collection by submitting false reports. As every revenue collection system presents opportunities for the unlawful diversion of collections, the RMM Team is well advised to review collection procedures in detail with experienced auditors, recommending action to tighten up procedures, where indicated.

C) **Delinquency**. In cases of persistent delinquency, the RMM Team should review the arrears, account by account, and, if the responsible officials are lax in pursuing these delinquents, recommend vigorous action to collect amounts outstanding, and to forestall new delinquencies.

3) **Population Change**. In general, revenues relate directly to population size, that is, increase when population increases, and the reverse. But, the impact of population changes may not affect every revenue proportionately. For example an expansion of the number of very young people in urban settlements may not have the same impact on entertainment tax revenues as adults. Consequently

VI. PRELIMINARY WORK

the RMM Team should examine all revenues for the applicability of the population factor. To establish population projections, the RMM Team should consult planning officials. To determine the revenue impact of population changes, the Team must quantify the relationship between population aggregates and particular revenues, establishing per person correlations, such as, movie tickets per person, restaurant meals per person, etc. These correlations can then be applied to population projections to derive object and subject data which can be used to calculate the amount to be attributed to population changes.

4) **Change in Real per Capita Income**. Changes in real per capita income have an impact on many revenues. For example, as incomes rise, people tend to increase their use of restaurants, and travel more, using hotels. This tendency increases hotel and restaurant sales tax revenue, if that tax is properly added to each bill and the proceeds faithfully remitted. As increases in real wealth work their way through an economy through "multipliers," the RMM Team should consult knowledgeable economists in assessing the impact of this factor on revenues clearly subject to its influence.

5) **Change in Currency Value**. Changes in the value of currency, usually inflation, will automatically affect revenues with rates based on a percentage of the value of subject transactions, provided prices are not controlled by the jurisdiction. To apply an inflation/deflation factor to

price-sensitive revenues requires that the RMM Team determine an estimate of inflation/deflation for each year of the five year projection. As with Factor 4, consultation with knowledgeable economists is advised.

6) **Rate Changes**. This factor includes the revenue impact of changes in rate policies, and, most importantly, changes in rates to reflect the impact of changes in the value of currency on those taxes, fees and service charges which are fixed amounts related to objects and subjects, rather than prices. These revenues are not price-sensitive unless made so by deliberate and timely action changing rates. Failure to adjust rates to reflect inflation is a very common policy failure in many governments. Consequently, the RMM Team must give this factor strong attention, and reflect its resolve in its proposed action proposals.

7) **New Developments**. This factor encourages the RMM Team to consult with relevant officials to identify the character and timing of revenue-related developments over a multi-year projection period.

8) **New Revenue Sources**. This factor encourages the RMM Team to explore new revenue possibilities.

9) **Procedural Changes**. This factor encourages the RMM Team to explore the impact of rules, regulations and procedures other than those related to rates, which, if changed, could result in increased revenues and/or their more timely receipt.

VI. PRELIMINARY WORK

These considerations will help provide revenue estimates for the upcoming year and the ensuing years embraced by the jurisdiction's multi-year projections. It should be noted that revenues are "dependent" variables, that is, the amount collected is a "resultant," traceable to the behavior of "controllable" and "uncontrollable" environmental, policy and managerial variables. Consequently, the staff assigned to revenue estimation should first examine the context of each revenue, then formulate projections which 1) reflect the influence of "uncontrollable" factors (population, inflation, economic activity), then add the estimated value of policy and managerial action.

Recognizing the critical importance of management, the RMM Team should conduct an annual review of the management aspects of revenue collection. This review requires the RMM Team to assess the efficacy of revenue-related planning and monitoring practices throughout the jurisdiction. Management considerations include 1) the organizational complexities of the revenue collection process, 2) the special management requirements of revenue collection, and 3) the importance of time in collecting and depositing revenues. Once institutionalized, the management environment is fundamentally shaped by the requirements of the RMM process, especially its data demands and action timetables. Each year, the RMM process must produce the following key products:

1) Coverage Studies
2) Cost of Collection Studies
3) Cost of Service Studies
4) Rate Revision Proposals

The first three procedures provide a solid basis for attaining the fourth, the most important of all RMM events: updating the regulations governing taxes, fees and service charges.

Incorporating research findings and recommendations, the annual RRM Report should be a comprehensive document. Regarding projections, the revenue commentaries included in the Resource Mobilization Methodology Report should reference tables displaying the collection histories and multi-year forecasts, making it possible for readers to maintain a perspective when reviewing the research findings and recommendations. Projection assumptions and methodology require accurate, complete documentation.

As previously stated, and repeated here for emphasis, formal work plans and periodic performance reviews provide the best response to efficacy concerns. Consequently, in conducting its research on the management aspects of revenue collection, the RMM Team should apply instruments of performance measurement. Further, officials charged with revenue collection duties should strive for effectiveness, efficiency and economy by maintaining data arrays which quantify the relationship between input and output. These relationships can be best quantified by formulating performance ratios, or unit measures. These measures provide a foundation for work plans, an essential basis for monitoring revenue collection activity. The monitoring process must not be left to chance and circumstance. Periodic performance reviews are required to evaluate the status of listed activities, and to authorize corrective action to maintain progress, when indicated. The staff of centralized revenue collection units and the staff of revenue-collecting service units should be provided periodic opportunities to report (a) performance for the current milestone period, (b) revised estimates for the current period, and (c) projections for the coming period.

Task 2. Estimate Financial Capability

What might a Multi-Year Financial Capability Statement look like? Statement essentials are presented by means of two illustrations. These examples apply to a jurisdiction's general or consolidated fund, assuming that capital investments are recorded and controlled by means of a separate accounting entity dedicated to that purpose.

VI. PRELIMINARY WORK

Exhibit 6.5 outlines a format for the content of an annotated statement of key facts and assumptions affecting the composition of a Financial Capability Statement. It lists topics which might merit recognition as factors affecting the projection of a government's financial capability. Requiring careful and thoughtful consideration, a statement of projection assumptions and facts represents a key contribution to the development of a jurisdiction's fiscal and budgetary perspective.

Exhibit 6.5. Facts and Projection Assumptions

	TOPIC	SPECIFICATION	NOTES
A	Population		
B	Gross Domestic Product		
C	Budget Constraints		
D	Revenue Factors		
E	Loan Factors		
F	Program Cost Factors		
N	Etc.		

Exhibit 6.6 presents a model worksheet for the calculation of multiyear financial capability. It assumes the entry of estimates formulated by the team assigned to formulate an annual Revenue Mobilization Methodology. Exhibit 6.6 provides three columns to register projected revenues and expenditures for the upcoming budget and the following two fiscal years. If desired, the projection can be extended to cover more than three future years, although this step is not recommended. With tolerable degrees of error, government officials may be expected to project revenues and expenditures for a two-to-three year period, but no longer. Also, if desired, the model can be expanded to display the experience of prior years. However, from my point of view, historical experience should be excluded because its inclusion tends to encourage "mechanical" approaches (extrapolation) to projection, a tendency to be resisted. Projection techniques will be addressed momentarily.

Budgetary Thought for Budget Officers

Exhibit 6.6. Worksheet: Multi-Year Financial Capability

	GENERAL FUND	Current Year Estimate	Budget Year	Budget Year +1	Budget Year +2
1.0	RESOURCES				
1.1	Prior Year Balance (Surplus or Deficit)				
1.2	Base Revenue Projections* (List Sources)				
1.3	Subventions, Grants, Donations, etc.				
1.4	Other Resources				
	Total				
2.0	RESOURCES APPLIED **				
2.1	Operating/Maintenance Expenditures				
2.2	Debt Service				
	Total				
3.0	ESTIMATED BALANCE (Plus/Minus)				
4.0	ESTIMATED BORROWING POWER				
5.0	ADD CONTINGENT RESOURCES ***.				
	(List Sources)				
	Total				
6.0	ESTIMATED BALANCE				
7.0	ESTIMATED BORROWING POWER				

Notes:
* Base projections do not reflect any proposed rate adjustments, changes in management practices, or new taxes, service charges, fees, etc.,

** Capital Investments are assumed to be charged to a Capital Investment Fund, or some such separate accounting entity. Additionally, Capital Investments should not be incorporated in this table as their very authorization may depend on the amount of available funds (surpluses) and or finance (borrowing power) determined by the entries and calculations of this table.

*** Estimates assume the implementation of revenue policy and management proposals formulated by a Revenue Mobilization Team

Line 1.1 registers the estimated surplus or deficit carried forward from prior year operations. Of course, at the time of its calculation at the mid-point of the current year, the estimated surplus or deficit

VI. PRELIMINARY WORK

figure carried forward as available for funding the Budget Year will be the amount derived from the difference between estimated current year revenues and expenditures, posted on line 3.0 of the Worksheet. The same procedure applies to the two ensuing years. Significantly, the Worksheet displays revenues under two aspects, one projecting the *status quo*, (line 1.2), the other, possible changes in revenue policies and rates (line 5.0). Line 1.2 records revenue estimates for all four years referenced by the Worksheet. Revenues for the Budget Year and the two following years are to be projected using current policies and rates, with the proviso that they may be adjusted for anticipated changes in economic conditions which might affect collections. These calculations provide a revenue base for the Budget Year and two following years.

Lines 1.3 and 1.4 provide for the entry of estimates of subventions, grants and donations from other governments and parties, and funds flowing from miscellaneous sources not already entered in the table. As they are generally difficult to predict, conservative estimates are definitely in order here.

Concerning an expansive Line 2.0, Resources Applied, sufficient space should be provided to list estimates for operating and maintenance expenditures assigned to a jurisdiction's General Fund, identified by function, agency, etc. In best practice, these estimates are formulated by the responsible program officials. These officials should base their projections on current programmatic concepts, production techniques, and expected economic conditions. Obviously, these estimates, although projecting the status quo, may require adjustment for anticipated changes in economic variables, such as wage and price changes which increase costs without changing programmatic concepts or production techniques. Line 2.2 provides for the entry of the annual cost of servicing outstanding debt.

The worksheet provides two "bottom line" numbers which are of vital interest to all who are contributing to the anticipatory process. Line 3.0, identified as Estimated Balance, registers the amount derived by subtracting applied resources (expenditures) from estimated resources. This calculation produces a surplus or deficit. Obviously, surplus amounts may be made available to finance initiatives explored during the anticipatory planning process. Line 5.0, entitled Contingent Resources, records the incremental revenue effects of recommended policy and management actions (adoption of new forms of revenue, intensified enforcement, expansion of coverage, rate revisions, etc.) having a predictable impact on the timing and amount collected in the Budget Year and the two ensuing years. Obviously the adoption of these recommendations increases the support which might be made available for the funding or financing of initiatives to be considered during the anticipatory planning process.

Entries identified as Estimated Balance on Line 6.0, reflect the addition of resources which might be made available through revenue policy and rate changes. These are contingent resources. However, as the proverb warns, "there is many a slip between the cup and the lip," initiatives to be supported by these additional resources should also be identified as contingent on adoption of the recommended changes in revenue policies and rates. Lines 4.0 and 7.0 permit the registration of the results of calculations related to potential borrowing, before and after the addition of additional resources, respectively. In this model, uncommitted balances, or portions thereof, are used as indicators of amounts available to pay annual loan principal and interest on new debt. Of course, the total new debt which can be supported by these amounts depends on the amortization schedule, the interest rate and the debt coverage ratio policy of the government.

Exhibits 6.5 and 6.6 provide a model for the form and content of Multi-Year Financial Capability statements, subject, of course, to modifications stemming from differences in circumstances and budget and accounting concepts from jurisdiction to jurisdiction. Also the anticipatory process will undoubtedly produce proposals which alter the assumptions used to project revenues and expenditures. Indeed, it may be expected that the survey phase of the process will address questions

VI. PRELIMINARY WORK

related to the efficiency and/or effectiveness of existing government services. The Perspective should include an updated Multi-Year Financial Capability Statement, complete with entries recording the estimated impact (plus or minus) of expenditure and revenue recommendations.

Thus far, the discussion has centered on resources that pass through the government treasury: revenues, loan receipts and disbursements. Of course, cash resources are important, but the scope of an assessment embraces the entire government environment, private as well as public. Indeed, its wide scope is a distinguishing feature. The research team cannot properly address issues, problems and opportunities without considering the deployment of private resources which may be linked to the exercise of government power. From a strategic point of view, it does not matter who provides the good that is sought, as long as it is provided in a manner that is legally compliant. Without doubt, the assessment process can, and should, be used to encourage private parties to cooperate with one another, and with the government, to attain desired community goals. Finally, the assessment team may also recommend program and/or procedural changes, including regulations, which have strategic merit, but do not have budgetary implications to any observable degree.

An annual inflation assessment provides a case in point. Certain government revenues are inflation-sensitive, that is, with a rate expressed as a percentage, revenues increase with price increases. In contrast, revenues governed by set amounts, such as service charges, are not inflation-sensitive. Given the historical impact of inflation on government purchasing power, and the likelihood of inflation in the future, annual recommendations for increasing rates on all non-inflation-sensitive revenues can certainly be justified. But, the resistance to annual across-the-board increases in service charges may be strong. Recognizing resistance, the assigned staff might properly consider the strategic advantages of staggering the submission of recommendations for inflation-justified rate adjustments over a period of years, thereby gaining a better chance of legislative adoption. Similarly, in seeking to close serious cost recovery gaps, staff assigned to revenue mobilization might consider the strategic advantages of securing a general agreement to step-by-step increases in the percentage of costs recovered in designated service charges until a satisfactory relationship is attained in a designated future year.

Typically, officials are executing a current year budget when they initiate the formulation of next year's budget. In many cases, the current year budget will be a source of concern. Unanticipated events, unavoidable delays and revenue shortfalls are to be expected. If they are serious, and deemed uncorrectable during the remainder of the current year, these current year implementation problems should be addressed, and therefore listed at the top of the research agenda as "Unfinished Business."

Task 3. Conclude the Anticipatory Process

At this point, the reader would do well to review Exhibit 6.3, *Elements of an Anticipatory Process* and the associated discussion. Clearly, to be useful in the budget process, findings and recommendations developed through an anticipatory process must be submitted to the chief executive's office in time to influence the content of the annual call for estimates. The amount of time and effort devoted to assessments and the formulation of initiatives necessarily varies, depending on the complexity of the issues, problems and opportunities to be addressed. The starting date must provide sufficient time to (a) establish the assigned team, (b) set a research agenda, (c) assemble and verify required data, (d) conduct the research, (e) formulate initiatives and (f) compose a report of findings and recommendations. Governments developing fiscal and budgetary perspectives for the first time are well-advised to start at least six months prior to the issuance of the call for estimates. The conduct of an initial anticipatory process will undoubtedly require more staff time over a longer period than that required once the assigned research team and its staff gains

VI. PRELIMINARY WORK

experience with the process. Once the process is thoroughly institutionalized, an experienced team and its staff should be able to formulate the annual update in approximately 3 months. Thus, a starting date of no later than the beginning of the third quarter of each fiscal year is recommended.

The development of a fiscal and budgetary perspective requires the cooperation of many parties. To obtain and maintain this cooperation, the jurisdiction's leadership must actively support the assessment process. The jurisdiction's chief executive can appropriately express this support by these steps:

1) Announce the establishment of an assigned team, its research agenda and timetable.

2) Conduct a review of the work in progress one month prior to the due date for submission of proposed initiatives.

3) In concert with legislative leaders, conduct a public review of the recommended initiatives prior to issuing the call for estimates.

With all key officials participating, the recommended management review (Step 2) and public review (Step 3) will serve to advise all interested parties, including the public, about emerging recommendations and projections, and their implications for the jurisdiction's service and development plans. The management review is important as it provides a forum for defining and solving any remaining problems in completing the fiscal and budgetary perspective.

The chief budget officer should submit a proposed research agenda to the government's chief executive for suggestions and concurrence. Prior to approval, the chief executive should consult with legislative leaders about the proposed research agenda, taking their suggestions under advisement. The documentation process should not be left to chance, or to the inclinations of the assigned staff. Lost or misplaced documents, computer file accidents, unintelligible work papers, etc., are ever-present hazards in any research effort.

To merit legislative and public support for its recommendations, the assigned staff must do quality work. As a general rule, quality work requires concentration on key tasks and topics. The assigned staff must balance its desire to do in-depth research on outstanding issues, problems and opportunities against the need to produce proposed initiatives for possible inclusion in next year's budget.

Essentially, the formulation and execution of creditable initiatives, year after year, requires a consistent approach to the annual research agenda. First, staff and time constraints will not usually permit the assigned staff to conduct a comprehensive annual program of in-depth studies — and do it well. Second, even if the assigned staff could conduct comprehensive studies each year, the submission of more recommendations than the policy leaders of the jurisdiction are willing to consider would (a) waste valuable time, (b) frustrate the assigned staff, and (c) tend to reduce the credibility of the fiscal and budgetary perspective process.

Documentation of the findings and recommendations of a Fiscal and Budgetary Perspective is the final step in an Anticipatory Process. The findings and conclusions of the Perspective should influence the content of the Budget Call, including any project and program initiatives deemed worth serious consideration for inclusion in the executive budget to be submitted to the Appropriation Authority. Possibly the Budget Call will reference a "budget constraint." This term usually refers to a limit, expressed as an allowable expenditure total, or deficit amount. This reference may also be expressed as a percentage of the estimated Gross Domestic Product. Practice varies, but the Budget Call may set expenditure ceilings for agencies and the overall budget. Needless to say, these would be subject to incremental and decremental adjustment during the actual formulation of the budget for submission to the Appropriation Authority.

VI. PRELIMINARY WORK

The development of an annual Perspective should, and likely, would have a significant impact on the subsequent budget formulation process. If pursued on an annual basis, the requirement for periodic composition would foster the development of supporting analytical and planning capabilities throughout the government. It is also a fair assumption that the requirement of periodic composition would inspire collaboration among government units and nurture the integration of data bases which tend to be fragmented, or non-existent. Although it need not be a complex, detailed document, a Fiscal and Budget Perspective should reflect the best data and thinking available to the jurisdiction. In addition to key programmatic officials, knowledgeable persons and interested parties should be invited to contribute formally to the process, as should consultants, when appropriate. Responsibility for the conduct of the research process and the production of the resulting draft is best assigned to the jurisdiction's chief budget officer. As a decision-related document, a Perspective places possible solutions to identified issues, problems and opportunities within a framework of expenditure and revenue projections. Thematically, a Perspective embraces:

1) Succinct assessments of issues, problems and opportunities.

2) Succinct assessments concerning the means of attainment. (Estimated available resources and resource constraints affecting the next fiscal year and beyond, matched to expenditure projections.)

3) Initiatives. (Agenda of programs and projects proposed for budget consideration, complete with tentative costs.)

A set of inter-related forms (or, if computerized, format templates) should be used to document initiatives. Recommended instructions governing the formulation and documentation of initiatives embrace the following tasks. (This array of topics for the formulation of budgets has been previously presented and discussed. It is repeated here for the reader's convenience.)

1) Define the problem(s) to be attacked programmatically.
2) State goals in practical, measurable, time-bound terms.
3) Identify collaborators and affected parties.
4) Identify conditions required for goal attainment.
5) Reference written work plans for executing the preferred problem solution(s).
6) Display proposed allocations in a results-oriented (rather than commodity) format.
7) Identify alternatives considered, but rejected, and why.

Addressing these tasks encourages deep and broad thinking. Presenting proposed initiatives in this format provides assurance that a proposed initiative is well conceived and worthy of consideration for inclusion in the budget call. The benefits of the suggested formulation and documentation topology are discussed in Part Five.

Preceding budget formulation, a fiscal and budgetary perspective, based on a jurisdiction-wide assessment of issues, problems and opportunities, serves to counter the conservative bias of the budget process by highlighting important considerations which should condition the budget for the coming year. Minimally, a well-crafted perspective would include an authoritative statement concerning the jurisdiction's financial capability based on a recommended revenue mobilization methodology. This component of an annual perspective may be expected to condition budget deliberations, especially if the jurisdiction is committed to compliance with tax and expenditure limitations. A brief cautionary

VI. PRELIMINARY WORK

note concerning projection techniques closes this discussion of fiscal and budgetary perspectives.

Those who use mechanical projection techniques tend to rely on spread sheet software to extrapolate past experience into the future, with no consideration of policy, management or environmental factors which affect the revenues and expenditures in question. Methods, such as, "regression," or the successive application of percentage rates of change, or fixed amounts, to base amounts, are widely used in preparing multi-year financing plans. Statistical software facilitates the application of the "least squares" method of projection. This method establishes a "trend line" for past events which can be used to chart future events of a similar nature. Although easy and fast, such methods of extrapolation are less preferred for the following reasons:

1) For many reasons, year-to-year changes in revenues and expenditures may vary significantly. In most cases, the cause of the variation is unique in time and place and will not reoccur in the future. Consequently, a "trend line" constructed to chart unique past experiences provides a weak basis for projection. At minimum, every data series should be closely scrutinized for rate of change issues, base changes and anomalous events, and adjusted accordingly.

2) Even if year-to-year changes in revenues and expenditures are relatively constant in a past period, extrapolation of this experience is only permissible if future conditions are expected to duplicate the past. Few situations meet this specification. Error in forecasting future conditions is usually traceable to unwarranted assumptions of stable conditions (*ceteris paribus*) or that desired or necessary

conditions will effervesce without deliberate intervention and effort (automatic *mutatis mutandis*). (I have incorporated the Latin terms for two pervasive sources of error in human thinking and decisions because exotic phrases better engage the mind. I strongly recommend that all budget officers internalize and actively apply the meaning and wisdom of these Latin concepts in their analytical work.)

3) Mechanical approaches to revenue estimation negate the management methodology herein recommended, which requires adoption and implementation of actions based on research into event-influencing factors. This point deserves re-emphasis: Reliance on mechanical means of projection should be strongly resisted by government leaders because their use sheds no light on what must, or can, be done to produce future revenues.

Proposed priority initiatives have the best chance of effective and efficient implementation, if the proposed programs and projects are 1) within the limits of estimated available resources, and 2) incorporated in annual budgets by means of regular budget processes. This latter requirement clearly establishes managerial accountability for implementation. This may include special organizational arrangements for implementation, such as, project teams and inter-agency "task forces."

In summary, what outcome justifies an investment of a jurisdiction's resources in the development of an annual fiscal and budgetary perspective? "Effective implementation of efficacious programs and projects" is the short, positive answer to this important question. Justification can also be marshaled by referencing well-known shortcomings of a budget formulation process that starts out by calling for proposals from agency leaders, who tend to forward subjective

VI. PRELIMINARY WORK

justifications rather than objective judgments. Weak, inefficacious policy and program implementation is acknowledged to be a key problem in government jurisdictions everywhere in the world. Indeed, at the time of this writing (2015), the world's governmental landscape appears littered with inefficient, uneconomic and ineffective projects and programs. Abundant evidence indicates that the programmatic distribution of government resources changes only incrementally from year to year. By its very nature, a budget formulation process lacking institutionalized criticism cannot present a strong defense against the authorization and re-authorization of inefficacious programs. Unquestionably, a budget formulation process that lacks a built-in "front end" assessment phase, as herein recommended, gives program officials an uninhibited opportunity to express their deep self-interest "in keeping what they have got and getting more." How could it be otherwise? These are serious shortcomings addressed by the implementation of an assessment-based anticipatory process.

VII. KEY TASK: ASSESSING the MERIT of ALLOCATIONS

Resembling "investigating magistrates," budget officers assess the merits of proposals by public officials to spend "other people's money." The courtroom analogy directs attention to requirements for 1) effective methods of inquiry, and 2) a magisterial disposition on the part of budget officers. (The ethical dimensions of a budget officer's work are considered in my concluding note.) In this part, we will explore methods of inquiry, especially the criteria that can (and should) be applied. Judgment implies thoughtful consideration of evidence. In the case of public budgets, evidence concerning merit is usually problematic, and, therefore, conclusions drawn must often be appropriately qualified.

Effectively, government policy is expressed through appropriations. Yet, fundamentally, an appropriation is an act of faith, an attempt by appropriation authorities to cause something certain in an uncertain future. Further, an appropriation, despite its apparent solidity when enacted, is merely somebody's estimate converted into a rule governing official behavior. The adequacy and accuracy of these estimates are abiding concerns of officials and citizens alike, and a source of much anxiety, indecision and manipulation. Arguments over the adequacy and accuracy of estimates are an endemic feature of the budgetary process. Amid this uncertainty, budget officers are professionally committed to minimize variances between cost estimates and the consequent actual cost experience. So, it is appropriate that we open this commentary on a budget officer's key task with a key injunction: Budget officers must underwrite their assessments of allocation merit with an appraisal of the quality of the estimates under scrutiny.

Budgetary "Facts"— Problematic at Best

Skepticism about reliability is usually the best policy, as the estimates that provide the warp and woof of public budgets tend to be erroneous. Applied art, science and mathematics can help, but can not eliminate judgment and the probability of error from the estimation process. The question, then, is not really one of accuracy, but of tolerable error. How can accountable officials reduce estimating errors to a tolerable degree of variation? Achieving accuracy in a total budget is a stronger possibility than achieving accuracy in details. The tendency to aggregate the overall budget from a mass of subordinate cost centers is an important step toward an accurate total because the inevitable plus and minus errors of a mass of estimates tend to cancel one another out. (This assumes that detailed estimates are carefully and honestly developed.) The whole mass of estimates thus tends toward zero variation. One of the secrets, then, of overall accuracy in budgeting is making many subsidiary estimates, each based on the best available data or sources.

Although budget estimates are truly the results of "educated guesswork," accountable officials strive for reliability by using the following estimating techniques:

The Requirements Approach. Officials relying on this approach assemble a "shopping list" of requirements (staff, supplies, equipment, etc.) for each budgetary topic, entering a quantity and a unit price for each requirement, multiply each quantity by its unit price, then add these products together to obtain summary figures. The requirements approach is very common. Indeed, one could say that the "shopping list" approach is "budgeting" for many public officials, particularly supervisors whose participation in budgeting is frequently restricted to listing and pricing

VII. KEY TASK: ASSESSING the MERIT of ALLOCATIONS

requirements. Certainly, if they ascertain that the accountable officials apply discounts for available inventories, reductions in payroll costs due to expected staff turnover and add sensible adjustments for price inflation, budget officers can be reasonably confident that the shopping list approach produces soundly conceived cost estimates. However, for all of its merits, the shopping list approach has a significant "downside" because its users tend to assume that budgeting is merely an exercise in the *price* of things, rather than a thought process about the *worth* of things. Further, is there any evidence that this approach is more accurate than abstract, statistically oriented approaches?

Extrapolation. Using this method, accountable officials derive a future estimate from current and past experience, arranged in a "time series." Typically, the revised estimates of the current year are plotted with the experience of prior years, looking for trends or stable patterns of variation. In the simplest and most popular form, officials derive budget estimates by casting up an estimated cost for current year requirements, let us say, office supplies, then add an amount to adjust for inflation. Of course, this assumes that the requirements in question remain relatively stable from year to year.

To plot trends and variations in a time series, officials can use a variety of procedures, including:

- Freehand description of a trend line drawn through selected points.
- Semi-averaging to determine points for a trend line.
- Simple averaging.
- Squaring trend deviations to describe a line of best fit.
- Moving averages to smooth out minor fluctuations of a time series.

- Exponential smoothing of points in a time series, reducing the influence of older data on the trend line projection.

During my experience as a budget officer with the City of Hartford, Connecticut, its budget process included extrapolation techniques applied to snow removal and flood control allocations. The snow removal allocation was based on 10 years of past experience, using an average of operational variables, including overtime hours, sand, salt, contract equipment and contract labor. Current cost factors were then applied to the average amounts. The budget commentary described using the mean of a 10-year time series as a way to minimize the variance of expenditures from allocations in a situation where the demand for services could not be predicted. Similarly, city officials averaged past experience to budget for the variable costs of its flood control program, where pumping operations vary unpredictably from year-to-year. Accountable officials frequently use time series information—such as a simple average of current and prior year experience—then adjust this figure to reflect expected changes in any of the underlying requirements, staffing, prices, pay plan adjustments, etc.

Correlation. Using this approach, accountable officials seek to identify and evaluate "independent" variables which condition, or "determine," expenditure and revenue levels. Correlations express relationships between two or more variables in quantitative ways. Correlation studies can be very useful because causal relationships abound in governmental programs. Budgets based on estimated costs of implementing the courses of action suggested by correlation studies have a strong justification. Most importantly, budgets based on correlation can be objectively monitored. Despite the obvious utility of correlation-based budgets, this approach does not appear to be commonly used in the calculation and justification of budgetary estimates. Obviously, reliance on

VII. KEY TASK: ASSESSING the MERIT of ALLOCATIONS

correlation-based budgets requires that officials possess requisite mathematical competence.

Closely akin to the correlation approach is the method of estimating by "factors." For example, officials who calculate and track performance ratios, such as unit cost, can derive costs from estimates of workload. With work loads estimated, budgeting becomes an exercise in multiplication, as output measures are multiplied by estimated unit costs to produce budget figures.

Budgeting by work load and productivity measures is a fast and efficient method of producing estimates, provided that the measures are valid and reasonably accurate. As noted in Part Six, *Preliminary Work*, the discussion of resources mobilization recommends an approach to revenue estimating based on the factors that generate and affect a given revenue. The advantages of using correlation-based modeling in the programming and budgeting of public services is explored at some length in Part Five, *Formulation and Documentation Guidelines*. In addition to speed, and sufficient accuracy, these approaches center attention on the relationship of expenditures and revenues to causal factors, work loads and public goals — key concerns of a budget officer in the never-ending battle for budget rationality.

The situation with regard to the accuracy of performance information is also problematic. Budget officers and accountants continuously work with figures representing money, usually subject to internal controls and audit review. Data concerning results, however, is almost always non-monetary data. This data is unique to the program or project in question, and is almost always developed and recorded by the concerned program or project staff. This latter characteristic tends to render performance data suspect, especially to finance and budget officers, because it is collected and presented by officials who have a compelling interest in "looking good." In most governments, performance data is captured "catch-as-catch-can," stored in ad-hoc filing systems and occasionally related to expenditure and revenue reports by program leaders. Typically:

- It is program and project personnel who count, register and report events deemed useful in evaluating performance. Records are developed and kept at work sites.

- Performance data (even if computerized) is entered in ledger-like records and stored in on-site files, These files include original source documents, data compilations and copies of performance reports.

- Reporting and tabulation errors are rife in such "uncontrolled" recording and filing "systems," especially in those where money and audit reviews are not involved. .

Associating fees and/or service charges with performance indicators is an effective way to ensure the validity of performance data, because where money is involved, reporting procedures will fall under the scrutiny of accountants and auditors. With the fee schedule known, revenue reports can be organized to provide evidence of the volume of use, service or activity. Additionally, if performance data can be made subject to internal accounting controls, responsible program managers will be much more likely to foster the use of mechanical and electronic counting devices, and establish and enforce administrative controls, such as, double entry or cross-footed data recording, and tabulations and calculations which increase fidelity and reduce the possibility of error.

The problems associated with performance data can be mitigated, if officials are willing to take steps to guarantee data validity, such as, strictly enforced internal controls on the collection of data, independent

VII. KEY TASK: ASSESSING the MERIT of ALLOCATIONS

surveys, sampling studies and field audits. Because performance data is so difficult and expensive to validate, few governments even try. Further, with reference to strict application of the above-cited criteria, one must not expect more precision than the subject matter allows, a wise observation of Aristotle. Certainly, it is fair to state that the expense of validating performance data is deemed a sufficient deterrent by most governments to inhibit the development and maintenance of credible performance data arrays.

Of course, concerns about the integrity of budgetary information are heightened when expenditure proposals are brought under critical review. While data deficiencies can often be redressed on short notice, under pressure, a continuous interest in the validity and reliability of budgetary data is obviously the better practice. Although the budgetary data base is inherently problematic, budget officers must ever seek to improve its quality. Expenditure estimating techniques can be taught. Officials whose estimates are consistently unreliable can be put to school. Practices and procedures can be examined for their affect on estimation. Advice can be issued by knowledgeable authorities on commodity prices and inflation expectations. As previously pointed out, associating fees and/or service charges with performance indicators can help to ensure the validity of performance data, because where money is involved, reporting procedures will fall under the scrutiny of accountants and auditors. With reference to revenues, the mobilization procedures recommended in Part Six, *Preliminary Work*, can help to produce valid, reliable estimates.

In sum, budget officers, no less than accountants and auditors, have abiding concerns about data integrity. But, concern is not enough. Principled leadership and action is required. As the custodians of the budget process with a vital stake in the quality of budgetary data, budget officers have a compelling reason (and duty) to initiate and sustain systematic measures fostering the validity and reliability of expenditure and revenue estimates, and associated performance data. Here, as always, an ounce of prevention is worth a pound of cure. In this regard, prior to the call for estimates, budget officers should conduct training sessions for all program officials with responsibility for budget formulation and implementation, with special attention to those newly appointed to supervisory positions.

More on Essentials: Performance Data Articulation and Use

Obviously, standing alone, proposed expenditures do not provide a basis for an appraisal of their intrinsic and relative merit. As with all things, meaning is provided by relationships. In public budgets, allocations are best invested with worth when related to an appropriate array of performance indicators that are effectively used by accountable officials throughout the budget cycle, specifically during budget formulation, adoption and implementation. Savvy officials know that capturing performance data, interpreting it properly, then effectively using it will enhance their reputation for competence. Obviously, this stress on effective use of performance indicators subjects the budget process, itself, to a performance test, that is, the accountable officials must show that they are using performance indicators to allocate and implement budgets. This axiom directs attention to the critical role of official leadership in the successful employment of the techniques of results-oriented budgeting. Bluntly put, given the essentially problematic nature of "performance" by public service agencies, it takes persistent, principled official leadership to make results-oriented budgeting, itself, perform.

(An author's aside: Truly a variable, "leadership" differs radically from administrative and accounting practices which can be institutionalized with assurance that their prescriptions will influence behavior in desired ways. Leadership is a personal, rather than an organizational attribute, inherently idiosyncratic. However, the exercise of desired leadership action is not completely dependent on the vagaries of fortune. Leadership behavior can be

VII. KEY TASK: ASSESSING the MERIT of ALLOCATIONS

taught and learned, as proven by the careers of military and business school graduates, and the cadre of city managers providing non-partisan leadership in localities with the council-manager form of government. Ultimately, as human action of a desired kind rests on congruent belief, official action favoring performance data articulation and use depends on internalized ideas and ideals. To express principled leadership, accountable officials must be inspired to champion performance data articulation and use even when so doing can damage reputations and deflate egos. It is this author's hope that this "what-to-think-about-it" book will have this desired inspirational affect.).

Typically governments employ many officials who, by inclination and vested interest, resist any accountability system they cannot control. Identifying appropriate performance indicators and overcoming resistance to their effective use requires officials who relentlessly devote time and attention to the definition, collection, validation and dynamic use of performance indicators. Given statistical probabilities, the desired leadership attribute will not be uniformly possessed by the members of any sizable cadre of accountable officials. Officials naturally rising to this desired standard of behavior do not occur in great numbers. Recognizing the problematic nature of performance in public programs, governments choosing to employ results-oriented budgeting, and succeed at it, have no choice but to support this choice by investing in administrative and accounting procedures that foster the desired leadership behavior, including systematic training and technical assistance programs provided to the entire cadre of supervisory officials.

Accumulating experience indicates that officials who wish to use performance data in adopting and implementing budgets face a variety of impediments - a spectrum of endogenous and exogenous difficulties found in legislative and administrative situations everywhere. The following commentary explores this critical problem, suggesting organizational and procedural solutions.

Essentially, an appropriation represents a legislative act of faith. In adopting budgets, appropriation authorities *assume* a rather linear relationship between their programmatic intentions and eventual results. Or else, why bother! For the mathematically minded, the production function of public budgets can be expressed algebraically by the, $y = f(x)$. In this equation, y equals the output, outcome or impact resulting from the application of x amount of resources, using various production techniques. However, it is well known that the presumed production function assumed by an act of appropriation is frequently indefinite, and its operational effects problematical. The experiments with various forms of results-oriented budgeting represent attempts to specify the relationship between the programmatic intentions assumed by an act of appropriation and eventual results. As indicated by the following list, the relationship of appropriations to results can be, and is, addressed in a variety of ways:

- Most common practice: Reflecting administrative agency requests, program documentation and testimony, legislators appropriate in good faith, assuming that desired results, variously understood, will be forthcoming

- Appropriations are authorized in increments, contingent on demonstrated performance

- A substantial "base" appropriation is initially authorized, followed by incremental allocations, contingent on demonstrated performance

- Independent objective/subjective ratings of agency performance influence legislative consideration

VII. KEY TASK: ASSESSING the MERIT of ALLOCATIONS

of agency budget requests and subsequent appropriation allotments by administrative authority

- Improvements in performance are rewarded with increased funding. (Assumes that public agencies normally perform sub-optimally, unless stimulated)

- Uncommon practice: Appropriation amounts and the underlying program intentions are influenced by the systematic application of formal allocation criteria, such as performance ratios, investment returns, marginal productivity calculations and mathematical models

For all who are interested in the effective budgetary use of performance information, the last point in the list is the most desirable practice. Ideally, the relationship between appropriations and results should be reciprocal and dynamic, that is, appropriations should result in the anticipated results. In turn, results should influence the behavior of management and appropriation authorities. In reality, as noted by a legion of interested observers and practitioners, appropriation authorities (and, regrettably, many administrative officials) have not been noticeably impressed by presentations of operational results. Otherwise, how can one account for the frequency of instances where funds continue to be provided in the face of manifest performance disappointments and outright programmatic failures?

One likes to think that legislators (and administrative officials) place a premium on attaining anticipated results for funds expended. They often do not! Nevertheless, it would be rash to attribute legislative inattentiveness to sheer indifference. Generally, legislators do care about appropriation effectiveness. However, this concern is usually superseded by more pressing legislative considerations shaped by partisanship and the pressure of special pleas from socio-economic formations. And, as is well known, the agents of those formations interested in appropriations can be counted on to devalue and discredit performance data when indicated results may affect future budget allocations. Also, many legislators can be counted on to protect favored programs from performance-based criticism. Further, and even more disappointing, administrative agency leaders have been known to excuse, devalue and discredit negative operating results. Finally, as in all things legislative, the attitude of legislative leaders toward performance data and interpretations is a crucial factor. Legislatures lacking leaders who champion program efficacy (effectiveness, efficiency and economy) are not likely to develop and sustain a constituency interested in the budgetary use of performance data. When and where it occurs, legislative disinterest in the budgetary use of performance data and interpretation is not only a serious procedural deficiency, but undoubtedly reduces administrative enthusiasm for the managerial use of performance data. Stating this thought positively, legislative attention to performance begets administrative attention to performance. Interested observers and practitioners have also been concerned about administrative disinterest, attributing the lack-luster performance of administrative officials in the managerial use of performance data to foot-dragging and studied indifference. Indeed, it is a rare government that does not harbor officials, who, by inclination and vested interest, resist any accountability system that may report results potentially damaging to egos and future budgetary support.

To reinforce the key point previously made: Given the problematic nature of performance in public service programs, only persistent, principled official leadership, expressed through supporting institutions, can make results-oriented budgeting, itself, perform. Consequently, governments seeking to employ results-oriented budgeting are well advised to invest in, and enforce, administrative and accounting procedures specifically centered on the a) definition, b) collection, c) validation, and d) dynamic use of performance indicators. How best to attain firm institutionalization of these four inter-related actions?

VII. KEY TASK: ASSESSING the MERIT of ALLOCATIONS

Performance indicators range from descriptions of specific events and items to abstract concepts. They also vary in conclusiveness — ranging from indicators identified with "instrumental" program activities to indicators describing final programmatic "end-products." Instrumental performance indicators are very valuable because they provide the rationale for the formulation and execution of work plans, especially in complex programs where several interdependent units and/or processes are contributing to the attainment of a single end result. As they tend to identify specific countable events or items, instrumental performance indicators are not usually controversial. Given the problematic nature of performance in public service programs, however, one can frequently expect interested parties to challenge the representativeness, validity and measurability of indicators describing programmatic end-products, especially when indicated results may negatively affect budget allocations. Nevertheless, it is clearly better to identify "end product" indicators, and suffer controversy, than to have none at all. It is equally obvious that effective performance concepts and related data must be logically associated with programmatic activities. Therefore, program documentation provides the best source of performance concepts which will command respectful attention from significant actors in the budgetary drama. Embedding performance information in budget documentation is the first and most basic step of institutionalization. This vital matter is explored in detail in Part Five, *Formulation and Documentation Guidelines*. In particular, consult Exhibit 5.1, *Formulation Topics and Documentation*, which provides an annotated list of suggested topics for the documentation of results-oriented budgets.

And mark this well: Conducting periodic formal performance reviews of work plans formulated by all supervisors is the best way to validate performance indicators that will prove useful in budget formulation, adoption and implementation. Distinguished from the passive practice of after-the-fact reporting, the dynamic use of performance data serves to illuminate the conceptual problems and issues which bedevil the process of performance articulation and usage under the best of circumstances. To qualify as "dynamic," the reviews should be conducted "before-the-fact," that is, 2/3rds of the way through the current reporting period. So timed, the reviewing officials have time to authorize "corrective action" in cases of impending failure of work supervisors to meet targets. Consequently, in addition to providing the entire performance articulation process with a compelling rationale, the active use of performance data during budget implementation encourages and supports desired managerial behavior.

Although program managers may actively resist performance evaluation, a policy of passive resistance is most likely. Obviously, only persistent managerial leadership can ensure the faithful performance of key procedures throughout a jurisdiction. Experience suggests that this leadership commitment must be supported by special staff assignments, and vigorous follow-up, to authoritatively express the jurisdiction's commitment to results-oriented budgeting.

An Essential Checklist: Allocation Criteria

No less than choices in everyday life, budgetary choices rest on applied criteria. As suggested by Exhibit 7.1, *Allocation Criteria,* public officials can tackle the problem of budgetary judgment *pragmatically* (subjectively) and/or *formally* (applying analytical techniques on principle). The ensuing discussion follows the order of Exhibit 7.1.

VII. KEY TASK: ASSESSING the MERIT of ALLOCATIONS

Exhibit 7.1 Allocation Criteria

PRAGMATIC CRITERIA	FORMAL CRITERIA

INERTIA
(Organizational and programmatic continuities)
 	
COMPLEMENTARITIES
(Services supporting other services)
 	
DISEQUILIBRIA
(Correcting imbalances; redressing grievances; restoring conditions)
	SERVICE STANDARDS
	Market Equity
	Equal Allocation of Resources
	Equal Results
	
	PERFORMANCE RATIOS
	Efficiency
	  Cost/Results
	  Results/Cost
	  Work Time/Results
	  Results/Work Time
	Effectiveness
	  Goal Attainment Percentage
	Programmatic
	  Unique Production Ratios
	
	MODELING
	Correlation
	
	INVESTMENT RETURNS
	Marginal Productivity
	Investment Yield
	
	WEIGHTING AND SCORING
	Ordinal Ranking
	Multi-dimensional Scoring

But first, a general observation: It is universally recognized that purely subjective criteria exert tremendous influence on the formulation, adoption and implementation of public budgets. Indeed, during the budget formulation process, administrative officials inevitably express their programmatic (and their self-interest) in their allocation proposals. And, typically, during the budget adoption process, legislative leaders invoke partisan loyalties to encourage legislative members to heed their budgetary advice. However, aside from providing interesting anecdotes, examining the role of purely subjective criteria in the budget process would not be productive because the application of subjective criteria is unique in every case. As unique events, it is not likely that knowledge about the application of subjective criteria can help legislators improve the quality of their budget decisions. Aside from a brief discussions of the budgetary influence of three key forms of pragmatic criteria (inertia, complementarities and disequilibria), this commentary on the meritorious allocation of public resources concentrates on criteria to be applied on principle, that is, applied, and the results respected, regardless of subjective evaluations and desires.

Administrative and legislative officials should strain toward the "best" distribution of the capital they may be able to drain from the economy in taxes, loans and fees. However, no matter how some would wish it to be so, governments are not businesses. With profit maximization as their goal, business leaders possess a widely accepted criterion of investment merit: the highest rate of expected return on allocated capital. Although government officials can sometimes apply a monetized investment return criterion to certain programs and projects, in most cases, they must lean on other criteria to weigh the comparative merit of various spending proposals, seeking the "best" distribution of public funds. The meritorious allocation of public resources is herein advanced as the "gold standard" of budgetary behavior. It is the singular concern of budget officers.

In the absence of authoritative budget formulation requirements, those officials charged with budget formulation enjoy considerable discretion in selecting, applying and disclosing allocation criteria. They are, so to speak, "judges of first instance," and, as such, bear the fundamental responsibility for the application and interpretation of assessment criteria. Serving as "judges of last resort," appropriation authorities have the fundamental responsibility to appraise the standards of judgment supporting proposed allocations, assuming that budget formulators have, indeed, applied pertinent criteria and have disclosed the results in

VII. KEY TASK: ASSESSING the MERIT of ALLOCATIONS

relevant budget documentation. If budget formulation and documentation is found wanting in this vital aspect, this shortcoming seriously compromises review of proposed budget allocations by accountable officials, budget officers and appropriation authorities. The "bottom line:" all officials charged with assessment tasks in the budget process should strive to understand and consistently apply objective standards of judgment. (In other words, do a better job at their job.)

Exhibit 7.1 classifies allocation concepts by the headings, *pragmatic* and *formal*. This division is a necessary concession to the real world of public budgeting – the world of selective evaluation and restricted options. At any given time, a very high proportion of proposed expenditures may be appropriately called "inescapable recurrent expenditures." Further, a very high proportion of proposed budgets are legislatively adopted with little serious criticism, or amendment. This recurring phenomenon attests to the power of pragmatic criteria, identified in Exhibit 7.1 as *inertia, complementarities and disequilibria*.

In practice, budget officers and legislators do not have enough time, even if they had the inclination, to conduct a thorough, even-handed review of all budget proposals. A strategy of selective evaluation permits them to impose a certain degree of order on a situation comprised of numerous documents, hundreds, perhaps thousands of numbers, and a plethora of competing values. If they can not look at everything, what do they look at? While actual practice varies, qualified observers report that budget reviewers tend to concentrate on large and/or increasing "discretionary" expenditures. In addition, they tend to skew their attention toward expenditure proposals which solve immediate, rather than remote problems, deal with familiar, concrete things and avoid probing into the programmatic values underlying proposed allocations, especially if they support established programs.

The conservative policy implications of a selective evaluation strategy are clearest in the tendency to assume that large portions of the annual budget represent "uncontrollable" expenditures. This well-nigh universal tendency to accept a significant proportion of spending proposals without rigorous review surely reflects prudence. It is also tacit acknowledgement that the time and expense of critical reviews would represent poor, perhaps futile, investments of time and scarce analytical resources. Knowledgeable observers go even farther by pointing out that untimely analytical attacks on popular programs—programs which are defined as "basic" or "vital," or programs regarded as "sacred cows" by powerful interests can produce negative returns for officials because their judgment is questioned. The resulting loss in credibility is often regarded as too high a price to pay for quixotic attempts to challenge the *status quo*.

To be fair, budget officers should not be accused of timidity if they avoid investing time and attention in reviewing expenditure proposals where little or no decision-making discretion exists (for example, debt service or other specific amounts required by law). However, as many observers have pointed out, expenditures which are objectively discretionary are often treated as if they were mandatory. In other words, labeling expenditure, "uncontrollable," is all too often an act of discretion by participants in the budgetary drama.

Lest pragmatic criteria completely dominate the budgetary process, all concerned (elected officials, administrators and citizens) should strive to enlarge the role of *formal* allocation criteria in budgetary decisions. On a scale of responsibility, legislative support for this desirable objective counts the most, at least theoretically. Indeed, in terms of positive impact on administrative behavior, the requirement for effective legislative demand cannot be over-emphasized. As a practical matter, however, experience with results-oriented budgets over the years indicates that legislators, in general, are not eager to apply objective allocation criteria in adopting appropriations, or to demand that administrators do so. Consequently, by legislative default and by professional commitment, the task of enlarging the role of formal allocation criteria in budget determinations falls to budget officers.

After definitions of pragmatic (subjective) allocation criteria, we will explore formal (objective) criteria, which, if applied on principle and with sufficient enthusiasm, can help accountable officials counter

VII. KEY TASK: ASSESSING the MERIT of ALLOCATIONS

the powerful tendency to apply pragmatic criteria, narrowing the scope of their application.

Pragmatic Allocation Criteria

The decision-influencing power of inertia, complementarities and disequilibria is undeniable. Applying one or more of these terms to any given budget allocation endows it with a certain subjective form of merit in the eyes of ever-pragmatic officials. Each is discussed, as follows:

Inertia. As a rationale for adoption, the force of "inertia" is given great weight in legislative deliberations. This phenomenon accounts for the relative stability of budget allocations over time, and the reluctance of legislators to reduce established services. And why not? The inertial factor reflects the very essence of government. (This phenomenon also accounts for the low appeal of budgeting approaches which raise serious questions about existing service policies, "zero-base" budgeting, for example. After all, governments are supposed to assist and stabilize society. To do so requires a significant degree of organizational and service continuity. Consequently, a very high proportion of proposed government budgets fund existing bureaucratic formations for another year of operations. And of this amount, a very high proportion is devoted to funding staff costs. For many legislators, these two purposes provide sufficient evidence of merit, as they may be loath to do anything, but complain, about the cost of established public services. The ready renewal of their annual funding, albeit amended, testifies to the inertial power of established bureaucratic formations, a the services they provide. In contrast to this tendency to accept the "base" of proposed budgets, legislators typically show a lively interest in incremental changes (usually additions). Of course, proposed increments to any given base budget, once adopted, fade into the base presented in the next budget cycle. The result is appropriately called "expenditure creep," a relentless upward trend in budget totals over time.

Complementarities. Allocations which support other allocations are also given great weight. A government of general jurisdiction will include many programmatic units dependent on service from central process agencies whose specialists service all units. Finance, personnel, legal, engineering and maintenance functions are typically established as central process agencies. Adding or expanding particular programmatic services indirectly puts pressure on intra-government supporting services. The concept of complementarity applied to budgeting attests to the web-like nature of government activities. As a rule, appropriation authorities tend to support expenditure linked to other approved expenditures, or to decisions previously made, e.g., operating and maintenance expenditures related to opening a new public facility. Requirements for documentation are noted in Part Five. See Exhibit 5.1, Statement 3, *Collaborators and Affected Parties*, for documentation requirements concerning complementarities. Budget officers have a special responsibility to closely review relationships between budget allocations, especially those supporting the service delivery capabilities of centralized process agencies serving programmatic units.

Disequilibria. Further, governments are expected to respond to the perceived problems of society, e.g., natural and socio-economic disasters, crime waves, income disparities, traffic congestion, etc. Therefore, they tend to support expenditure proposals designed to help correct perceived

VII. KEY TASK: ASSESSING the MERIT of ALLOCATIONS

inequities and imbalances affecting various interests in their social and economic environment. By their very nature as democratic institutions, legislatures are disposed to respond, especially when disturbances affect large numbers of people. Additionally, a plethora of relatively minor "concerns" arise to enliven every legislative session, whether it be the Congress of the United States, a state legislature, city council or special district governing body. Evidence of constant pressure to address problems agitating the citizenry is seen in the volume of legislation introduced by legislators prohibiting some form or other of citizen behavior deemed harmful by somebody or other. The vast majority of these initiatives die during the legislative process, but a sufficient number with budgetary implications are adopted to justify identifying disequilibria as a significant pragmatic criterion.

Formal Allocation Criteria

To re-emphasize, all concerned (elected officials, administrators and citizens) should strive to enlarge the role of formal allocation criteria in budgetary decisions. As a vital step toward that goal, Part Five recommended guidelines for budget formulation and documentation, assuming that the programmatic information so assembled would help budget officers to assess the intrinsic and relative merit of proposed allocations.

> **Intrinsic Merit.** A proposed allocation may be said to have *intrinsic* merit if its estimated programmatic effects and affects satisfy objective criteria, principally, the desired tendencies of the performance ratios listed in Exhibit 7.1.

Relative Merit. A proposed allocation may be said to have *relative* merit if its estimated effects and affects are deemed more valuable, on objective grounds, than those attributed to potential competitive allocations. Obviously, selecting proposed allocations to be made subject to such comparisons is a key decision, which should, if possible, reflect the application of objective criteria. Selection criteria might include, for example, all allocations involving requests for a) added staffing, b) expenditure increases exceeding a set amount or percent, or c) "overtime" payroll payments. Once a grouping has been determined, investment returns and weighting and scoring criteria can help to assess the relative merit of proposed allocations.

Exhibit 7.1 lists five approaches to formal evaluation which can be applied (on principle), to assess the merit of proposed allocations. It should be noted that, in contrast to the easy application of pragmatic judgment to expenditure aggregations, the employment of formal allocation criteria requires significant mental effort and performance data.

Service Standards. The criterion of service standards gives proposed allocations due weight if the estimated programmatic effects and affects clearly comply with stated mandated (legislative) programmatic objectives. To be sure, all public services utilize a working methodology, although it may not reference an acknowledged "service standard." Further, even when working methodologies are regulated by reference to standards, the impact of proposed allocations on mandated service delivery may be vague or obscure.

VII. KEY TASK: ASSESSING the MERIT of ALLOCATIONS

A cautionary note: As public expenditures are regarded as expressions of public policy, budget reviewers tend to ascribe merit to proposed allocations that they believe implement authoritative or "accepted" service standards. Obviously, budget officers and appropriation authorities should validate referenced standards. More important, even when proposed allocations are justified by reference to valid service standards, budget officers should not forgo lines of inquiry exploring the relative efficacy of alternative service philosophies. "Authoritative" service standards are established by legislative enactment. Strictly speaking, legislation authorizing the provision of public services should include standards of implementation. Indeed, setting standards of service demonstrates a high order of legislative responsibility. "Accepted" standards are sanctioned by traditional practice or technical requirements. In an outstanding example of adherence to tradition, for many decades in its history, the United States Government adopted "balanced budgets," although not required to do so by the Constitution. Widespread municipal government acceptance of fire defense specifications advocated by fire insurance interests is an example of technical standards affecting budget allocations. Unquestionably, legislatures have the authority to adopt standards for the provision of public services, or to require administrators to do so. In practice, although they possess the right to prescribe standards for the provision of any service they authorize, legislatures frequently avoid so doing, most likely to provide program administrators with operational flexibility. As a case in point, lawmakers may prescribe the duties of a department of public works for maintaining public ways, but forebear establishing standards for that maintenance, such as those regulating street cleaning services displayed in Exhibit 7.2, *Examples of Service Standards.*

Exhibit 7.2 Examples of Service Standards

	MARKET EQUITY	EQUAL EFFORT	EQUAL RESULTS
EDUCATION	Per student expenditure is proportional to fees paid.	Per student expenditure is same for all students in the jurisdiction.	Per student expenditure is differentially allocated until all students are at, or above minimum performance standards.
PUBLIC WAYS	Frequency of street cleaning is proportional to taxes paid.	Frequency of street cleaning is same for all streets in the Jurisdiction.	Frequency of street cleaning varies according to the amount of litter.

Most assuredly, variations in street cleaning service standards entail differences in cost. Also, Exhibit 7.3 provides an example of alternative standards which might be applied to govern the formulation, adoption and implementation of budgets for educational services. In recent decades in the United States, equity standards related to public school finance were a prime topic of official concern at all levels of government.

Depending on type, expenditure classifications can help or hinder legislators seeking to identify service standards supported by budget allocations. Budget formats which focus legislative attention on expenditure objects such as salaries and commodities, hide, rather than spotlight the relationship of proposed allocations to service standards. In contrast, policy and performance oriented classifications direct attention to proposed expenditure aggregations related to service standards. However, as previously noted, establishing that a proposed allocation is justified by an authoritative or accepted service standards does not relieve the assigned budget officer of responsibility to assess merit by applying performance criteria, especially the efficacy triad.

VII. KEY TASK: ASSESSING the MERIT of ALLOCATIONS

By far, budget documentation is the best source for up-to-date information about the relationship of proposed allocations to service standards. Exhibit 5.1 in Part Five relates to this point as it lists recommended budget formulation and documentation criteria, numbered as statements. The first statement, concerning program rationale, requires justification of the activities to be funded by the proposed budget allocation. Further, Statement One requires the identification of key variables and cause and effect relationships (correlations) between key variables and desired results. Obviously, implementation standards qualify as key factors in a program justification.

Appropriation authorities usually display keen interest in program standards (as do interested parties). Unquestionably, legislators having access to budget documentation complying with the requirements of Statement One will be better able to identify the connections between proposed allocations and service standards. It is also clear that legislators who vote appropriations with little or no associated text indicating policy intentions are (consciously or unconsciously) delegating the power to define service standards to those officials charged with budget implementation. Suffice it to say that effective, conscientious legislators perceive the importance of specifying standards of service to govern the formulation and adoption of public service budgets.

In best practice, legislators should use their power to require that the responsible administrative officials apply formal criteria, appropriately drawn from the available repertoire, when formulating budget proposals. Further, the analytical process used in budget formulation should be disclosed in pertinent budget documentation. This is the first and most efficacious line of effort for legislators interested in adopting budget allocations which have been subjected to objective tests of merit. The secondary line of effort requires questioning accountable administrative officials by legislators, referring to the repertoire of formal allocation criteria.

Performance Ratio: Efficiency. This popular measure, in the same manner as the other measures listed in Exhibit 7.3, *Concepts and Desired*

Tendencies of Unit Measures, is produced by dividing performance measurements by measurements of effort (cost and work time data), and the reverse. A desired tendency for each measure is also listed. Unit measures are very useful. Arrayed in a time series, these ratios facilitate objective evaluation of production techniques.

Exhibit 7.3 Concepts and Desired Tendencies of Unit Measures

	UNIT MEASURE	DESIRED TENDENCY
X/Y	Cost (X) per unit of measurable results (Y)	DOWN
Y/X	Units of measurable results (Y) per cost (X)	UP
Z/Y	Work time (Z) per unit of measurable results (Y)	DOWN
Y/Z	Units of measurable results (Y) per work time (Z)	UP

Notes:
"X" Equals "cost."
"Y" Equals output/outcome/impact, monetized if possible. If not, specified in numerical or physical terms.
"Z" Equals effort, defined as work time in terms of hours, days, weeks, etc.

However, we must quickly note that in periods of currency devaluation (inflation) the cost of doing business increases, often causing unit costs to rise, despite managerial efforts and improvements in production technique. Obviously, this circumstance undermines the evaluation utility of unit costs, unless adjusted for inflation. Consequently, calculations based on work time are to be preferred. Unaffected by currency degradation and responsive to changes in production technique and technology, a scheme of unit times (production per work hour or the reverse) is more revealing over time than calculations involving costs.

By definition, managers (including public program managers) should justify their production decisions by reference to the values of the efficacy triad, that is, effectiveness, efficiency and economy.

VII. KEY TASK: ASSESSING the MERIT of ALLOCATIONS

If benefits can be specified in numerical, physical terms for different production techniques, managers have a good basis for comparing alternative production techniques. Effectively, when administrative officials rely on performance ratios to inform their resource allocation decisions, they require the development and maintenance of performance measures and related measures of cost and effort— a wholly desirable state of affairs to be actively encouraged by budget officers. In reviewing budgets, budget officers (and legislators) should look for evidence that program officials are actively seeking to decrease the unit costs of program operation, increase output per work hour and enhance unique programmatic performance ratios. The latter ratios are shortly discussed.

Performance Ratio: Effectiveness. Ratios which relate performance measurements to targets are particularly valuable as they testify to program effectiveness. As an indicative example, 1000 high school students are enrolled in 10th grade classes. Two years later, 800 of these students graduate. Dividing the number graduating by the original 10th grade cohort produces an effectiveness ratio of 80%. In another example, in a given city with 1,000,000 dwelling units, its housing code program administrator estimates that 900,000 units are code-compliant. In this example, program effectiveness is an estimated 90%, leaving a performance gap of 10%. Proposals to increase effectiveness ratios (or close performance gaps) deserve close scrutiny as performance improvements are usually harder (and more costly) to obtain as effectiveness ratios near 100% — an effect well known as "diminishing returns." This aside, budget documentation referencing effectiveness ratios, if provided, certainly provides a good starting point for an assessment of the relative merit of proposed allocations.

Performance Ratio: Programmatic. The performance ratio concepts thus far discussed can be applied generally. The last concept identifies ratios that are programmatically specific. The well-known pupil/teacher ratio is an example of a relationship concept specific to education programming. In education allocation decisions, this ratio is given great weight by school authorities. In another example, per capita figures are frequently used in attacking and defending proposed allocations for a wide spectrum of government programs. Further, nearly all significant government program are dependent, in various degrees, on scientific, professional and technical personnel. The national societies of professional and technical personnel are important sources of programmatic performance standards and criteria. Ratios published by these societies abound. If judicially applied, with allowance for particular circumstances, legislators can use authoritative programmatic ratios to evaluate the substance and thrust of programs under review.

Modeling. Proposed allocations can be described by the linear equation, $y = f(x)$, which is mathematical shorthand for the production function of public budgets. In this equation, "x" equals the allocated resources, "y" equals output/outcome/impact, monetized if possible, if not, then specified in numerical terms, and "f" symbolically denotes the production technique, such as, police patrols, inspection, teaching, etc. This equation assumes that changes in applied resources produce constant corresponding changes in programmatic effects and affects — a linear conception of the budgeting process, accurate within limits. In most cases, however, the relationship between resources applied and results is not constant, and is best described by curvilinear, rather than linear conceptions of cause and effect.

The curve shown in Exhibit 7.4 represents a changing relationship between applied resources and results. Assuming a stable mix of resources and production techniques, the curve describes relatively low rates of program effectiveness (percent of goal attainment) at low levels of expenditure (x), sharp increases in rates of effectiveness (y) as expenditure rises, but declining rates of effectiveness for increased

VII. KEY TASK: ASSESSING the MERIT of ALLOCATIONS

expenditure thereafter. This tendency is popularly known as "diminishing returns." Reviewing proposed allocations through the lens of diminishing returns can result in locating cases where increased expenditure produces a) an increasing rate of performance improvement and b) after a certain point, no performance improvement at all. Thinking in terms of a curvilinear relationships between input and output variables, as graphically described by Exhibit 7.4, directs analytical attention to situations where the rate of performance improvement is stagnant at both ends of a curve of diminishing returns. Given that many government programs are marked by either under or over-investment, given the performance goals in view, identifying such situations can support recommendations to add or subtract resources, change the resource mix and modify production techniques.

The mathematical aspects of using equations in the assessment process are secondary to their conceptual utility. Their use provokes the right questions. Although data deficiencies limit the practical application of equations to the relationship between budget allocations and their effects and affects, their conceptual impact encourages budget officers to focus on varying relationships between input and output variables. Equations belong in every budget officer's tool kit.

Thus far this discussion of formal allocation criteria has emphasized the calculation of relationships between inputs and results, assuming rather simplistic connections between cause and effect. However, more often than not, public programs are complex activities. A well known example comes readily to mind: the dual function of the elementary and secondary schools, simultaneously providing "education" and "daycare" services, depending on one's viewpoint. One could advance more examples of causation and multiple effects in public safety, public health and other complex programs. Although linear relationships provide valuable insights into questions about the relative merit of budget allocations, accountable officials also need a way to explore complex programs. Budget officers and legislators charged with assessing the relative merit of proposed allocations for complex public programs, such as public education, public health and public safety, can enrich the review process by asking accountable program officials to identify the relative impact of different production variables on a desired result — an application of the concept of mathematical modeling. Computers have put mathematical modeling within easy reach of public officials, done in-house or commercially. Such systematic correlation studies illuminate the relative effects of variables thought to influence programmatic performance. Models define an ordered set of assumptions about causes, effects and objectives. By using models to specify relationships between variables thought to "make a difference," public officials can better advance their ability to attain and sustain a desired level of effectiveness. As hypothetical statements, models display an ordered set of assumptions about causes, effects and objectives.

For the sake of example, assume that accountable educators identify three variables affecting the performance of high school English students: 1) the verbal facility of the teachers, 2) performance feedback, and 3) parental interest. Each variable can be quantified and then assessed for relative impact by means of an equation designed to explore variables assumed to "cause" or "promote" student competency:

$$C = W_1(TVF) + W_2(PF) + W_3(PI)$$

Where:

C = Student Competency
W = Coefficients
TVF = Teacher's Verbal Facility Score
PF = Performance Feedback (Rewriting)
PI = Evidence of Parental Interest

Assuming that the verbal facility of the teachers is found to be the most influential variable, this finding should influence recruitment and retention practices, and associated allocations. The abstract nature

VII. KEY TASK: ASSESSING the MERIT of ALLOCATIONS

of models concentrates attention on important and effective program variables worthy of budgetary support. Their use helps administrators and legislators avoid distraction by peripheral issues and administrative trivia. Consequently, accountable officials should be familiar with the applications of mathematical modeling and encourage their systematic use in budget formulation and review.

Investment Returns. Theoretically, governments should invest in programs and projects yielding the highest comparative net benefit, monetized and discounted to present value to adjust for the effect of time on the value of money. Yield may also be calculated by dividing the measured benefit conferred by a program or project by its cost, expressed as a ratio. To quality as a viable investment, the benefit/cost ratio must exceed 1 plus an assumed discount (interest) percentage:

$$\frac{\text{Benefit}}{\text{Cost}} > 1 + \text{Discount \%}$$

With these ratios in hand, and ranked high to low, the proposed allocations in question can be comparatively considered for adoption. However, excepting application to government-owned enterprises and certain programs where results can be appropriately measured and/or monetized, the investment returns approach can not be used to evaluate the comparative merit of most government programs and projects.

Marginal Productivity. As previously emphasized, officials tend to avoid serious questioning of the budgetary base, concentrating instead on changes in proposed expenditure aggregations, especially increments. As proposed increments are assumed to be worth more than they cost, intellectual tools are needed to probe and test these claims. At this point, examine Exhibit 7.4, *Marginal Productivity*. It describes the "Law of Diminishing Returns." The concept represented by this graph can condition and enrich the budgetary thinking of all participants in the budgetary process. In Exhibit 7.4, the amount of applied resources would be scaled right-ward as increasing inputs on the horizontal axis, "X." The benefits, measured by output/outcome/impact quantities associated with the inputs, would be plotted accordingly, scaled on the vertical "Y axis"

Exhibit 7.4 Marginal Productivity

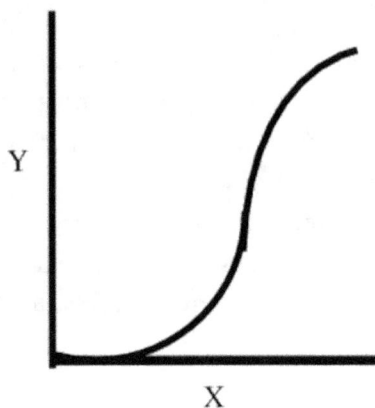

The amount of relative benefit rises most steeply in the mid-range of an expenditure pattern and tapers off as the amount of investment passes the point known as the margin, that is, the point after which each amount of additional expenditure results in a increased return, but at a decreasing rate. Finally, the returns to investment amounts reach the point where returns on increasing investments cease and may start to decline. Importantly, the concept of "marginal productivity" offers budget reviewers an approach to comparing disparate programs — the most intractable problem of budgetary evaluation. Within jurisdictions, every program represents a unique response to some perceived public issue, problem, or opportunity Given program disparities, program-to-program comparisons on programmatic grounds are not logically possible. As a popular saying has it: "You cannot compare apples with oranges."

VII. KEY TASK: ASSESSING the MERIT of ALLOCATIONS

So, even if it is not possible to directly compare the efficacy of dissimilar programs, it is possible to estimate proportional changes in marginal productivity, program-by-program. With comparisons reduced to percentage changes, budget officers can recommend shifting investments marked by the highest declining marginal productivity to those with the highest increasing marginal productivity. There is little doubt that consistent legislative (and citizen) interest in systematic marginal analysis would stimulate program administrators to seek and implement production techniques and the mix of resources which enhance program efficacy. Consult Exhibit 7.5, *Model for Marginal Productivity Comparisons,* for an indicative approach to the problem of relating changes in performance to different levels of investment. .

Exhibit 7.5 Model for Marginal Productivity Comparisons

ALLOCATION RATIO	IINCREMENTAL CHANGE	ESTIMATED PERFORMANCE
80% of Proposed Budget Allocation	20% Reduction in Proposed Budget Allocation. Presumes change(s) in program goal(s) and/or Production Technique.	Output/Outcome/Impact (Quantity)
100% of Proposed Budget Allocation		Output/Outcome/Impact (Quantity)
120% of Proposed Budget Allocation	20% Increase in Proposed Budget Allocation. Presumes change(s) in program goal(s) and/or Production Technique.	Output/Outcome/Impact (Quantity)

Weighting and Scoring. The simplest and most popular prioritization technique achieves a priority list by requiring officials to rank budget proposals by assigning numbers (1, 2, 3, etc.), or letters (A, B, C, etc.). These numbers or letters frequently represent the application of defined prioritization concepts, such as, urgent, essential, required, necessary, desirable, etc.

Exhibit 7.6 Weighting and Scoring Model

	Priority	Legally Prescribed	Increase Tax Base	Improve Results	Maintain Service	Expand Service
		0	1	2	3	4
Safety	1	0	1	2	3	4
Health	2	0	2	4	6	8
Education	3	0	3	6	9	12
Civic/Cultural	4	0	4	8	12	16
Convenience	5	0	5	10	15	20

VII. KEY TASK: ASSESSING the MERIT of ALLOCATIONS

Using the matrix, a proposal to expand a public health program, drawing a "2" from a list expressing public priorities and "4" from the list of allocation criteria thought important by government leaders, receives a final combined priority of "8." Please note that in this example, zero is assigned to legally prescribed proposals, putting them at the top of the list, regardless of other considerations. Also note that the rankings drawn from each list are multiplied together to produce a combined ranking. Because they serve to clarify and objectify values, weighting and scoring procedures help participants in the budget process to organize, but not eliminate, subjective judgments. In this regard, it is obvious that, using the lexicon of contemporary politics, the priorities of the model matrix reflect a conservative bias, favoring the values of the efficacy triad and limited government.

The illustration assumes that the accountable officials have agreed on two ordinal scales, with zero assigned to legally mandated services. With this agreement, each budget allocation can be tested against the values of the scheme, and its comparative rank established. For example, a proposal to build covered bus stops along certain arterial roads might be denoted as a "public convenience," meriting a "5" from the left-hand priority list. As this proposal might also be defined as a "service expansion," it draws a "4" from the horizontal scale. Multiplying them produces a single priority number, "20." Following this procedure, each proposed allocation, can be assigned to an appropriate group with a rank number from zero (mandated) to composite priority of "20." The lower the number, the higher the assigned priority. This methodology requires that expenditure proposals be aggregated by cost in priority group order until a total expenditure limit is reached. When the aggregation nears the limit, proposals in the affected priority group must be again prioritized for inclusion in the aggregate budget.

Obviously, weighting and scoring schemes organize - rather than eliminate - the subjective judgments of those involved in the budget process. This, however, is a major benefit because the establishment of the scheme itself encourages legislators, and other participants to clarify and objectify their values.

The effort to assess the intrinsic and relative merit of allocations helps to spotlight opportunities to displace program goals and/or substitute program procedures. It is widely acknowledged that public programs, and their procedures, tend to roll on, unchallenged and essentially unchanged, from year to year. In the heavily-weighted inertial environment of government bureaucracies, budget officers must aggressively promote the concept of *goal displacement and means substitution*. This is important work, as redirecting allocations from ineffective and/or inefficient programs to new initiatives enables governments to address new problems without additional taxes or loans. The disposition to relentlessly pursue opportunities for goal displacement and means substitution is a distinguishing mark of competent budget officers.

Assessing Merit

In jurisdictions with an executive budget system, following a call for estimates, program officials formulate and submit proposals for funding. This approach has great virtue as it ensures that budget estimates are formulated by officials most competent to do so. However, as virtues often have defects, this approach fosters the arts of advocacy, rather than critical thinking and analysis. As judges of first instance, it is not surprising that program officials assume that their proposed budget allocations are meritorious. Further, as interested parties, they tend to devalue and avoid applying objective tests of merit. And one must not forget that inertia and time constraints favor the advocates of established programs. Budget officer competence and will power is severely tested in the struggle against the inherent conservative bias of the budget formulation and adoption process.

Documentation requirements are the budget officer's first line of effort. Documentation requirements provide the principle means of counter-balancing the tendency of program officials to rely on inertia and argument, rather than evidence and logic, to win support for proposed allocations. As indicated by the discussion in Part Five, budget officers have a vital, abiding interest in budget formulation and

VII. KEY TASK: ASSESSING the MERIT of ALLOCATIONS

documentation format and procedure. The formulation process must be structured to produce evidence (and argument based thereon), logically organized, that enables budget officers and subsequent reviewers to assess the merit of expenditure proposals.

The topology listed by Exhibit 5.1 and its benefits, is repeated here for the convenience of the reader:

> The recommended documentation should 1) define the issues, problems and opportunities to be attacked programmatically; 2) state goals in practical, measurable, time-bound terms; 3) identify collaborators and affected parties; 4) identify conditions required for goal attainment; 5) reference written work plans for executing the preferred problem solution(s); 6) display budget allocations in a results-oriented (rather than commodity) format; and 7) identify alternatives considered, but rejected, and why,

The suggested topology confers four benefits. First, requiring accountable program managers to address each of these interrelated topics provides budget authorities with assurance that the requested allocation has been carefully considered and justified by evidence and logic. Second, requiring accountable officials to address each of these interrelated topics provokes consideration (thinking) and then composition of an appropriate text. Experience with this documentation scheme attests to its effect on the thinking of accountable officials, promoting the use of evidence and logic in the development of proposed budget allocations. Third, requiring program managers to address each of these interrelated topics provides an evidential base for dynamic implementation monitoring, facilitating the comparison of ongoing results against original intentions. Finally, the suggested typology provides a logical sequence for the presentation of budget documentation. Detailed specifications for the documentation topics are presented in Part Five.

The recommended formulation and documentation specifications are designed to encourage program officials to think critically, that is, use evidence and logic in problem analysis, goal specification, the evaluation of program impact or results, and the analysis of expenditure, workload and revenue relationships. In practice, from jurisdiction to jurisdiction, formulation and documentation specifications are known to vary widely in the breadth and depth of analysis required. However, even if expenditure proposals do not satisfy the recommended criteria, budget officers are well advised to use the topology, as defined above, to maintain control of their work during the press of the budget formulation period. The sample checklist presented by Exhibit 7.7 is based upon the recommended topology. Providing an "organizational memory," checklists can serve to anchor a process control system.

Exhibit 7.7 Documentation Checklist

Cost Center _____ Code _____
Accountable Program Official _____
Assigned Budget Officer _____

	STATEMENT	SATISFACTORY	
		YES	NO
1	Rationale		
2	Goal(s)		
3	Collaborators and Affected Parties		
4	Conditions of Performance		
5	Work Plan (Preferred Solution)		
6	Budget		
7	Alternatives		

Notes: _____

VII. KEY TASK: ASSESSING the MERIT of ALLOCATIONS

After reviewing submitted estimates for validity and reliability, budget officers should then test the submitted documentation for compliance with the standards advanced for each of the seven listed topics. This process serves to alert budget officers to data discrepancies and deficiencies. Put in question form, these discrepancies and deficiencies must be communicated forthwith to the concerned program officials. It is particularly important to have adequate program rationale and goal statements on all significant expenditure proposals. If submitted proposals do not meet the desired standard of documentation, budget officers should take immediate steps to get satisfactory statements from the responsible officials. Assuming that the requisite documentation is in hand, budget officers can proceed to examine expenditure proposals, applying indicia of merit. Obviously, an ounce of prevention is worth a pound of cure. As has been emphasized, budget officers should 1) school program officials in budget formulation and documentation before the issuance of the call for estimates, and 2) assist them in perfecting their proposals. In a well-ordered budget process, program officials should know the criteria of judgment, and the line of questioning to be applied by budget officers.

Using the checklist suggested by Exhibit 7.7, budget officers can quickly test discrete expenditure proposals for positive, negative and ambiguous conformance with pragmatic and formal criteria. As a general rule, expenditure proposals showing the desired effect of applying formal allocation criteria, e.g., increased output per work hour, deserve support, and the relevant officials, praise and encouragement. In those cases, where the result of calculations point in an undesired direction, e.g., higher unit costs, budget officers should encourage program modifications, such as changes in production technique and the mix of applied resources. Although suggested changes may require funding, budget officers should support initiatives related to desired efficacy tendencies, fiscal conditions permitting.

Indications registered on the suggested checklists can help budget officers maintain control of their time and effort during the brief period between the receipt of programmatic and project allocation proposals and the deadline for settling the content of the budget to be submitted to the appropriation authority. Checklists are useful in setting agendas for effective, efficient conduct of vital consultations, conferences and workshops with accountable program officials. If, during this period of questioning, budget officers do not get desired responses from program officials, they may recommend amendment of proposed allocations, justified by reference to the efficacy triad and other allocation criteria. Such recommendations should be submitted to the accountable program officials forthwith, giving them an opportunity to respond. Budget officer amendment recommendations should be specific, citing perceived problems and/or issues related to program goal(s), production techniques and resource mix.

As is often the case, perceived problems are not solved nor issues resolved in any given budget formulation period (at least to the satisfaction of the concerned budget officer). Consequently, reflecting experiences acquired during the budget formulation period and those gained during budget implementation and field trips, every budget officer should maintain a file of performance improvement projects to be pursued when time permits in-depth research. (An appropriate research methodology for budget officers is considered in Part Two.) Only decision-related assessments are possible during the period between receipt of proposed allocations and the final formulation of the chief executive's budget.

As repeatedly stated, a high proportion of proposed allocations support existing organizational and programmatic arrangements. These tend to be re-appropriated with no more justification than that they exist. Year to year, budgets tend to perpetuate allocation patterns, changing slightly in total, and even less in shares. Programs have inertia. *The inertia of currently funded operations is a most vexing problem of public budgeting.* That which has been given is hard to take away. Paradoxically, most budget officer are loath to waste their precious analytical time on entrenched expenditure patterns, yet these are probably

VII. KEY TASK: ASSESSING the MERIT of ALLOCATIONS

most in need of critical attention. Usually, program proponents classify their requests as "inescapable recurrent" expenditure even though, in many cases, program rationale may be weak, or weakening as times change. They tend to assume the very thing needing proof. Helping governments to address new problems without additional taxes or loans by redirecting allocations from ineffective and/or inefficient programs to new initiatives certainly ranks as a prime responsibility of all budget officers. By directing critical attention to relationships between input and output/outcome/impact indicators, budget officials can help reduce the power of inertia, and help rationalize allocation patterns.

Thoughts About Process Control

Unquestionably, determining the merit of proposed allocations is demanding intellectual work, executed under trying conditions. As noted. documentation requirements are designed to foster and facilitate program evaluation and planning, first by the agency officials requesting appropriations, and then, by budget officers who must testify to the relative merit of agency requests by recommending a budget to chief executives and thence to appropriation authorities. This work involves a sequence of steps implementing the key purposes of a budget formulation and adoption process:

1) Ensure the proper formulation of budget proposals and their timely submission.

2) Assess proposed allocations for intrinsic and relative merit and formulate recommendations thereon.

3) Compose and produce the chief executive's proposed budget.

4) Support the legislative process leading to budget adoption.

To ensure an orderly distribution and flow of work, the chief budget officer should assign subject matter and tasks to appropriately qualified budget officers. In jurisdictions with many programmatic agencies, the chief budget officer is advised to designate a "process controller" to establish and maintain the required process controls.

1) Documentation Review. As indicated by Exhibit 7.7 *Documentation Checklist*, budget officers, individually, are advised to establish process controls to govern their work. Budget office supervisors also need to establish overall controls to ensure that the formulation process is progressing efficaciously. Exhibit 7.8, presents a suggested process control chart governing the review of budget proposal documents. It provides for listing cost centers by code. As the content of each of the recommended seven budget proposal statements is certified as satisfactory by the assigned budget officer, the appropriate cell is checked. If kept updated, this chart enables the chief budget officer to assess the status of the formulation process at a glance, and initiate corrective action, if indicated.

Exhibit 7.8 Budget Proposal Process Control Chart

Code	Cost Center	Budget Officer	Statement						
			1	2	3	4	5	6	7
1	A								
2	B								
3	C								
"N"	"N"								

Budget proposal documents should be thoroughly reviewed immediately upon submission. If incomplete, mathematically inaccurate, or substandard in form, the assigned analyst should call upon the concerned agency for corrective action. All commentaries and exhibits should adhere to conventions established by the chief budget officer. Suggested conventions include the following:

VII. KEY TASK: ASSESSING the MERIT of ALLOCATIONS

- Each revenue source and expenditure cost center should be properly identified, and references to them in data arrays and commentaries standardized.

- All data arrays showing past, present and future figures should span similar periods.

- All tables should display uniform formats, applying a common methodology for numbering, titles, capitalization, abbreviations, column headings, notes, etc.

- When incorporated in specific revenue or expenditure commentaries, data drawn from data arrays should be consistently referenced,

- A consistent method should be applied when "rounding" numbers, including percentages,

- With regard to projections, to provide perspective, historical data should accompany any multi-year forecast.

- Also, with regard to projections, careful and complete documentation of projection assumptions and methodology is required.

As noted above, the budget proposal documentation requirements are designed to foster and facilitate program analysis and planning. These seven statements should provide data and interpretive commentaries which illuminate the relationship between resources (input) and expected results (output, outcome or impact).

Budgetary Thought for Budget Officers

The assigned budget officer must thoughtfully review this documentation for its analytical value. Do the statements adequately indicate what is to be done (output), or achieved (outcome or impact), when and why? Equally important, how are the projected results to be attained? If the documentation does not establish a clear and compelling relationship between resources and results, the assigned analyst shall provide accountable agency officials with comments and suggestions for revision.

> Most important, during the initial review, proposed budgets are to be carefully examined for satisfactory compliance with the provisions of the chief executive's call for estimates. In cases of questionable compliance, the assigned budget officers should immediately consult with the accountable program officials concerning a satisfactory response to instructions. Should the situation persist, non-compliance should be reported to the accountable officials for appropriate corrective action.

2) Assessment. Budget assessment is sequential, involving several levels of consideration. At the most basic level, assigned budget officers must seek to understand and assess the quality of the relationship of the requested resources (preferably incorporated and priced as "cost centers") to projected outputs, outcomes or impacts. To determine *intrinsic merit*, each relationship should be tested by reference to the criteria of the efficacy triad and service standards. Once satisfied with the merits of these relationships, budget officers may confidently apply criteria of *relative merit*, (Investment returns, marginal productivity and weighting and scoring), comparing the projected results of various allocations to one another, seeking the best overall mix of allocations to recommend for adoption. Beyond doubt, determining relative merit is the most challenging of all budgetary tasks.

VII. KEY TASK: ASSESSING the MERIT of ALLOCATIONS

As repeatedly emphasized, redirecting budgets from ineffective and/or inefficient programs to new programmatic initiatives should be a key allocation strategy of government leaders who wish to address new socio-economic problems without undue recourse additional taxes or loans. With reference to the listed allocation criteria, the budget process should be designed to encourage officials at all levels to expand the proportion of budget allocations justified by formal, rather than pragmatic allocation criteria. Attaining this strategic goal of the budgetary process requires the establishment and maintenance of productivity-oriented managerial environments throughout the jurisdiction. Therefore, budget officers must encourage and support program officials who are trying to increase the effectiveness, efficiency and economy of their operations. Conversely, program officials who fail to reference their operations to the efficacy triad deserve censure and justify negative funding recommendations.

Exhibit 7.9 Incremental Expenditure Analysis Worksheet

	Revised Current Year Estimate	*Amount*
Reasons for Difference (Plus/Minus)	+/-	
	Proposed Budget	*Amount*

Further, budget officers may wish to concentrate on expenditures, cost center by cost center, seeking to understand and evaluate the mix of requested resources, by type and quantity. Comparing resources proposed for the coming fiscal year to those funded by the current year budget provides a quick, efficient way to conduct an expenditure analysis. To document this comparison, a worksheet similar to that shown by Exhibit 7.9, *Incremental*

Budgetary Thought for Budget Officers

Expenditure Analysis Worksheet, will be helpful. This Worksheet provides spaces for recording the reasons for year-to-year changes in the type, quantity and price of resources to be allocated to a particular cost center. If properly completed, this Worksheet provides the assigned budget officers analyst with an answer to the frequently asked question, "Why are the proposed expenditures different from the estimated expenditures for the current year?" This "increase - decrease" approach is the most basic method of budget analysis. Although designed to illuminate year-to-year changes in expenditures, the analysis of expenditure also provides insight and data useful for program analysis – the process focusing attention on the relationship of proposed expenditures to performance.

Using the information provided by program documentation and the testimony of accountable program officials, assigned budget officers should be able to identify the relative role of resources and production techniques in attaining expected results. The mix of resources and production techniques are the keys to program performance. The important performance concepts are listed in Exhibit 3.5, *Performance Conceptions.*

During the process of formulation and adoption, budget officers should take advantage of every opportunity to acquaint accountable officials with criteria useful in the determination of the intrinsic and relative merit of proposed allocations of public funds. In the discussion of dynamic monitoring, I noted that the institutionalization of that essential process absolutely required vigorous support by budget officers. I can say the same about the responsibility of budget officers for the application of performance criteria. Their active commitment, expressed by precept and example, is absolutely indispensable. It is certain that if this commitment is absent, or weakly expressed, subjective judgments will inevitably rule the process of formulating and adopting proposed allocations.

3) Composition of Proposed Budgets Submitted to Appropriation Authorities. In jurisdictions with an "executive budget," expenditure and revenue recommendations must be approved by the jurisdiction's executive authority for incorporation in a budget submitted to its

VII. KEY TASK: ASSESSING the MERIT of ALLOCATIONS

appropriation authority. The composition and production of this budget is usually a responsibility of budget officers. In well-ordered jurisdictions, the submitted budget will reflect the reasoned programmatic and financial recommendations of budget officers. Further, budget officers are usually responsible for the budget's interpretative text, either as composers or editors. Finally, they are usually responsible for its production as a book and/or a downloadable electronic file. Although submitted budgets, published as "books," vary in format and content, they typically include a budget message from the chief executive, and sections for summaries, estimated revenues, estimated general operating expenditures and recommended capital projects. Depending on the legal requirements and customary practices, submitted budgets may include sections on programmatic and financial arrangements related to special purpose activities and government-owned enterprises.

The composition and production of submitted budgets are demanding tasks, executed under deadline pressure. Process controls are needed to ensure the composition of text, page by page, and the editing and proofing of all data arrays and interpretative text, including summaries. To establish control, the chief budget officer should establish a complete "mock-up" of the budget document to be submitted to the appropriation authority, section by section with composition and editorial assignments, page by page. The table of contents serves as the page control. As page form and content are certified as ready for duplication and binding by the designated budget controller, the appropriate page number is checked. If kept updated, this page control enables the chief budget officer to assess the status of the budget composition process at a glance, and initiate corrective action, if indicated. Agreement between the content of the chief executive's budget message and the content of the submitted budget must be assured by proofing arrangements.

4) Support for the Legislative Budget Adoption Process. Typically, legislators need and seek information and advice during consideration of proposed budgets. Also typically, there is no shortage of interested parties (program officials, lobbyists, special pleaders, etc.) willing to provide such assistance. Complex, and frequently confusing to all but legislative leaders, the budget adoption process is enlivened (and, hopefully, enlightened) by public hearings, subject-matter workshops and partisan debate. In larger jurisdiction, legislators may have access to specialized legislative staff units providing non-partisan, analytically-based advice and assistance. Generally, however, legislators are abjectly dependent on testimony from program officials and budget officers implicated in formulating the proposals under review. To many legislators, this situation is inherently unsatisfactory.

In well-ordered governments, the participation of executive branch budget officers in the legislative budget adoption process is regulated by their chief executive and chief budget officer, with unauthorized communication with legislators discouraged. Although budget officers are potentially valuable sources of information and assistance, they are usually limited to supporting program officials who are called to testify at legislative hearings and workshops. From an ethical point of view, this "behind-the-scenes" role may be a blessing in disguise, as it is not unusual for budget officers to be at some level of disagreement with their superiors and program officials about the merit of proposed allocations submitted to the legislature. The ethical hazard is clear. During the legislative budget adoption process, negative personal opinions expressed by administrative budget officers will surely be perceived as disloyalty. Yet, budget officers must be honest to maintain a reputation for integrity, a priceless asset. Thus, if questioned by legislators, the testimony of administrative budget officers relative to the merit of proposed allocations is best confined to programmatic and financial facts, referring requests for evaluation and opinion to program officials.

VIII. IMPLEMENTATION METHODOLOGY: DYNAMIC MONITORING

Essentially, adopted budgets represent an act of faith by appropriating authorities – an attempt to shape the future in desired ways. As such, appropriations simultaneously authorize, direct and limit the behavior of implementing authorities. As universal experience amply testifies, results often fall short of legislative expectations, if these be accurately disclosed via the form and documentation of appropriation acts. As public budgets have expanded in recent decades, program shortfalls and failures have attracted critical attention. Indeed, the history of budget reform can be interpreted as a struggle to achieve stronger causal connections between legislative intentions, if made transparent, and results, if also made transparent. Concentrating on the institutional foundations of budget implementation, the following discussion makes a case for dynamic, rather than after-the fact, monitoring.

Unquestionably, officials who wish to use performance data in adopting and implementing budgets face a variety of impediments – a spectrum of endogenous and exogenous difficulties found in legislative and administrative situations everywhere. The generally weak response of public officials to the implementation challenge is de facto recognition of manifest hazards and intrinsic difficulties.

As more and more of the world's financial resources are subject to budgeting by governments and an increasing number of not-for-profit organizations, the scope of the implementation problem enlarges. Overcoming impediments to effective budget implementation is especially important for democratic governments, which are inherently subject to more implementation impediments than authoritarian regimes. Authoritarian regimes have a survival stake in their effectiveness, and can use means not available to democracies to "make good" on their decisions. Consequently, in the continuing competitive struggle with authoritarian governments, democracies have a significant stake in finding ways to overcome budget implementation impediments.

By and large, participating officials find budget formulation and adoption exciting, even exhilarating. Not so with the process of budget implementation. As appropriations trigger work, fear and anxiety tend to replace exhilaration among accountable program officials, for it is fated that most government programs fail to attain promised results. Although the role of budget officers during the formulation and adoption phases of the budget cycle is well understood and rather standardized, their role in budget implementation is less so. Beyond examining and/or preparing allocation transfers and allotments (if used), the implementation role of budget officers varies from government to government, depending on monitoring arrangements. Indeed, one can go as far to say that governments that fail to deeply engage budget officers in monitoring will have a process that is fragmented, weak, even non-existent. Supporting this point, it is axiomatic that, without budget officer support and monitoring, allotment processes degenerate into meaningless accounting rituals, providing program leaders with little incentive to plan and perform. This is important because a ritualistic or non-existent allotment process usually correlates with a weak or non-existent performance monitoring system. As will be emphasized, an effective, dynamic monitoring system depends on active budget officer involvement for its effectiveness.

Implementation problems can be addressed by using "tools" readily at hand, but not usually found "working hand-in-hand." In administrative terms, these "tools" comprise inter-related procedures, which become "determinants" of successful implementation. These

VIII. IMPLEMENTATION METHODOLOGY: DYNAMIC MONITORING

determinants are 1) effective articulation and use of performance information; 2) an elaborate, flexible classification and coding scheme; 3) administrative and accounting procedures facilitating the aggregation of non-monetary performance data, formally correlated with measures of effort and monetary data; and 4) continuous management utilization of four inter-related instruments of budget implementation. These instruments include a) work plans, b) allotments, c) formal, periodic "before-the-fact" performance reviews and d) timely corrective action. Effective budgeting (efficient attainment of performance objectives) is best assured by using an institutional framework integrating these instruments, with accounting procedures providing the glue. The four instruments must be employed hand-in-hand, lest the absence or ineffective employment of one lead to reduced effectiveness and/or nullification of the utility of the others.

Budget officers are ideally positioned to actively implement and support a monitoring process aimed at identifying, authorizing and implementing timely corrective action in cases of impending goal attainment failure.

Obviously drawn from the bloodless realm of technique, each of these instrumentalities has a natural foundation in management practice, and can have an ideal development, *provided* accountable officials throughout the jurisdiction possess and express appropriate motivation and talent. This critical proviso spotlights the crucial role of skillful leadership.

The effective employment of the quartet of instruments noted above also depends on managerial energy and appropriate direction. At all organizational levels, officials must actively express a "will-to-achieve" in terms of the information produced by the monitoring process. Obviously, the "will-to-achieve" varies from official to official. Consequently, governments desiring effective conduct of results-oriented budgets (that is, efficient attainment of performance objectives) must take steps to ensure that their managerial cadres, especially those directly accountable for production, express requisite motivation and technical competence. In terms of desired characteristics, officials responsible for the formulation and implementation of results-oriented budgets should 1) crave a deserved reputation for productivity; 2) pursue goals based on research, work planning, and dynamic monitoring; 3) demand accountability for results from themselves, their colleagues and subordinates; and 4) promote innovation, training and organization development.

By textbook definition, "managers" relentlessly seek productivity. The officials of governments that practice result-oriented budgeting assume (consciously or otherwise) that, sufficiently encouraged and supported, public officials can become "managers" actively pursuing productivity. This assumption locates the "cause" of productivity in the managerial environment, rather than in managers, per se. In business organizations, the objective reality of economic survival permeates all work environments. In the public service, however, lacking the spurs of profit and competitive pressures, productivity will not effervesce unless consciously (on principle) cultivated by leadership and design. Standing alone, results-oriented budgeting will not automatically produce systemic productivity. Additional administrative mechanisms specifically targeted on productivity are required, especially systematic programs of training and technical assistance, working within a periodic performance review system.

"Before-the Fact" Formal Periodic Performance Reviews

Unless strong monitoring procedures are institutionalized, budgeting amounts to an annual estimating ritual, supported by accounting practices. More than any other part of the budgeting repertoire, it is the institutionalization of formal, periodic "before-the-fact" performance reviews which invests a budget system with "managerial muscle." When conducted as formal affairs, dynamic monitoring sessions tend to stimulate desirable organizational behavior, as follows:

VIII. IMPLEMENTATION METHODOLOGY: DYNAMIC MONITORING

- Anticipation of periodic formal performance reviews influences supervisory behavior during the intervals between reviews.

- Conduct of the review, itself, influences behavior as the participants reach understandings and agreements concerning actions to be taken by particular parties.

- Reviews identify "corrective action" by supervisors of units "upstream" of the unit under review that can help solve productivity problems defined during review proceedings.

- The reviews stimulate accountable officials to initiate "corrective actions."

Effective organizations attain stated goals. Efficient organizations attain stated goals at "minimum or lowest" cost. Effectiveness and efficiency are relative concepts which acquire meaning only through comparisons. Assessing the effectiveness and efficiency of any person or unit requires the development and maintenance of data, and data arrays, as follows:

- Effort devoted to stated intentions, expressed in terms of money and work-time.

- Results related to stated intentions, expressed in terms of output/outcome/impact indicators.

- Calculations dividing effort by results, or results by effort. (performance ratios)

- Additional productivity measurements or ratio(s) based on a comparable situations, providing reference data. for evaluations.

To be readily available for work plan formulation and the subsequent performance reviews, the required performance data must be (1) identified, and (2) recorded. As incurred, costs and work time must be associated with appropriate activities and/or tasks identified in work plans, then summarized at pertinent milestones. Similarly, output data must be recorded and summarized. Over time, using performance as a guide, responsible officials will be in a position to encourage the formulation of plans to improve the relative effectiveness, efficiency and economy of program operations. "Performance" is similar to the terms, "efficiency" and "effectiveness" in that it requires comparison to give it significance, or meaning. In the following abstract calculation, significance is given to a stated "performance" by deriving a "variance" by subtracting an ideal, standard or target from it, both stated, of course, in similar terms:

$$\frac{\text{Performance}}{\text{(Ideal/Standard/Target)}}$$
$$\text{Variance}$$

In plain language, a variance equals actual results minus planned results. These terms can be absolute numbers, or unit measures or other performance ratios. In addition to revealing the magnitude of variance, the subtraction will provide an indication of the direction of the variance in that the stated performance will equal (=), exceed (+) or fall short (-) of the stated ideal, standard or target.

Performance reviews provide formal opportunities for supervisors to address the officials and units influencing their ability to attain their goals, presenting a) results compared to intentions for the completed prior period, b) revised estimates of results related to intentions for the

VIII. IMPLEMENTATION METHODOLOGY: DYNAMIC MONITORING

current period and c) projected intentions for the upcoming period. The projections also form a solid basis for allotment requests and for cash management planning.

By design, the reviews should be conducted by strategically constituted Performance Review Committees 2/3rds of the way through the current reporting period.

So timed, with 2/3rds of the period completed, responsible officials have sufficient experience to calculate revised estimates for the current period, conditioned on proposed action plans for the remaining 1/3 portion of the period. These timely reviews provide the government with sequential opportunities to ensure goal attainment by encouraging, and/or authorizing timely corrective action in those cases where results are falling short of targets. At the 2/3rds point, if the projected unfavorable variances are deemed significant, the accountable officials still have time remaining in the period to authorize corrective action (adjusted staff deployments, changed procedures, etc.) to put the performance for the period "back on target."

As recommended, formal performance reviews provide supervisors periodic opportunities to address their colleagues and superiors concerning their performance, no later than every quarter. Ideally, supervisors should provide a "stand up" presentation, supported by visual aids, when appropriate. All presentations should reference the commitments registered in the current work plan, with significant variances indicated and explained. In general, experience indicates that supervisors will trace variances between intentions and results to one, or more, of the following factors:

a) Unanticipated changes in input prices.

b) Unanticipated changes in volume and type of applied resources, including staffing.

c) Unanticipated performance from assigned physical assets.

d) Unanticipated and uncontrollable changes in the production situation which invalidate original production assumptions.

e) Environmental contingencies.

Variances in unit measures are frequently traced to factors "a" and "b." In an economy subject to inflation, unanticipated cost variances are to be expected, as prices cannot be accurately predicted, even for the near future. Factor "c" is often cited to explain variances from period to period, especially if new technology has been introduced. Equipment failure, and/or delays in equipment repair also frequently cause negative variances. Significantly, factor "d" considerations often include shortfalls in services and/or goods due from other units of the government. Factor "e" refers to accidents, including natural and man-made disasters, which interfere with the conduct of work.

VIII. IMPLEMENTATION METHODOLOGY: DYNAMIC MONITORING

Exhibit 8.1 Performance Review Specifications

- Formal performance review procedures are to be established by regulation.

- All officials who supervise the work of others are to be provided with a forum for oral, written and visual presentations.

- To provide supervisory officials with a supportive audience, reviews are to be conducted by Performance Review Committees whose members are to be selected for their ability to assist supervisors to attain stated targets.

- To provide opportunities for corrective action when failure to attain target(s) appears likely, reviews are to be conducted periodically, 2/3rds through established reporting periods.

- Reviews are to cover prior reporting period (results related to intentions), current reporting period (estimates related to intentions), and next reporting period (projection of intentions).

- Budget officers are to serve as Performance Review Committee secretariats. Theses administrative duties include documenting proceedings and reporting thereon to accountable officials regarding status of targets and recommended corrective actions.

Work plans require adjustment as the work proceeds. As dynamic documents, revised work plans should always register the latest current estimates of work time commitments and output delivery dates. Therefore, performance reviews provide an opportunity to assess progress, and, if necessary, adjust future work time allocations, and, perhaps, output delivery dates. As indicated by the requirements displayed in Exhibit 8.1, these reviews are to be treated as formal occasions, with the staff assigned to each activity/task granted appropriate time for presentations.

In recommended practice, budget officers should be assigned the responsibility for organizing and coordinating the performance review process. The following steps are required:

1. Appointment of Performance Review Committees.
2. Designation of Committee chairperson and secretariat.
3. Arrangements for time and place.
4. Timely notification to all participants.
5. Provision of projection equipment and audience seating.
6. Conduct of the review.
7. Preparation of the Review Committee Report.

This recommended procedure supplements the normal process of meetings between subordinates and superiors concerning production problems. Such "in-house" meetings are often a waste of time because the superiors involved lack access to the resources needed to address emergent production problems. An institutional approach, as recommended, gives supervisors access to a wider range of resources than commanded by their immediate supervisors.

In sum, performance reviews expose the fallibility of plans, for whenever intentions are compared to results, variances are the rule. Consequently, cost and work time overruns and missed deadlines are to be expected. Considering the inherent fallibility of plans, all participants in performance reviews should strive to maintain a positive, rather than punitive, atmosphere – avoiding fault-finding and criticism in favor of problem-solving and corrective action.

Work Plans

Performance responsibility is best secured by the formulation and execution of work plans, reviewed and updated periodically, no later than

VIII. IMPLEMENTATION METHODOLOGY: DYNAMIC MONITORING

quarterly. Although they have proven merit at all levels of government organization, work plan formulation and execution is especially useful at basic levels of organization and supervision, the points of service and product delivery. *As they list primary activities and tasks, work plans should be prepared by every official directly accountable for the work of others.*

Exhibit 8.2 Work Plan Concept

	Performance Element	Periods				Total Cost	Total Hours	Total
		1	2	3	4			
1	Activity/Task – Work Hours							
	Cost							
	Output							
	Performance Ratio							
	/__ /							
N	Activity/Task – Work Hours							
	Etc.							
	Total Work Hours							
	Authorized Absences – Hours							
	Total Paid Hours							

Work plans provide a foundation for periodic formal performance reviews, an indispensable ingredient of results-oriented budgeting. Work plans can be organized by days, months, quarters, etc. By tracking progress, a work plan-based review process permits the implementation of timely corrective action in all cases of impending failure to reach stated targets set for the period in question. The failure to formulate work plans, and to conduct periodic performance reviews thereon, represents a very serious management deficiency.

The preparation of a work plan, and the expenditure requirements to fund the activities and/or tasks set forth, represent the final step in the process of formulating and documenting a results-oriented budget, that is, a budget formatted to link input to indicators of production. The steps preceding the formulation of a work plan, and its associated expenditure requirements, should clarify the program rationale, state the goal(s) to be attained, identify collaborators and affected parties and specify the conditions of performance. If these steps are properly executed, work plans, and the associated expenditures, will have a firm programmatic justification. At minimum, work plans embrace the following elements: a) Activities/Tasks; b) Effort, expressed in work hours, and, if available, costs; c) Targets, expressed in terms of outputs/outcome/impact indicators; d) Checkpoints or Milestones; and e) Performance Ratios. Schematically, these elements can be arranged as shown in Exhibit 8.2.

Work plans may display data discretely, period by period, providing totals in the last column at the right. As an alternative, one may display data cumulatively, with each period's data added to the prior period. Consequently, each period provides a year-to-date total, with the last period's figures also serving as the year-end total. If desired, both formats, the discrete periodic totals and the cumulative year-to-date approaches, can be used simultaneously to provide maximum insight during the review process. General procedures for work plan formulation follow:

1. Identify work activities/tasks assigned to each cost center.
2. Identify and quantify desired output units associated with activities/tasks
3. Determine and list the input units (work hours, kilowatt hours, transportation, etc.) and other resources (e.g., contracts) needed to attain the expected results. .
4. Estimate input unit prices.
5. Multiply the required input units by their unit prices.

VIII. IMPLEMENTATION METHODOLOGY: DYNAMIC MONITORING

6. Price the other required resources.
7. Determine the total cost center allocation by adding all effort/cost components.
8. Where applicable, calculate unit cost or cost per unit of output.
9. Where applicable, calculate output units per work hour or work hours per output unit, and any other pertinent performance ratios. The following exhibit displays the desired tendency of selected ratios:

    Cost per unit of output should go............ DOWN
    Output units per cost should go................... UP
    Staff time per unit of output should go.... DOWN
    Units of output per staff time should go....... UP

10. Compare all ratios to past and current experience. If comparisons do not show movement in the desired direction, review production techniques and associated inputs, seeking improvements in productivity and/or lower input or work hours and/or costs..

Inevitably, work plans require adjustment as the work proceeds. As dynamic documents, work plans should always register the best current estimates of work time commitments and output delivery dates. Therefore, performance reviews provide an opportunity to assess progress, and, if necessary, adjust future work time allocations, expected output, and, perhaps, output delivery dates. These reviews will provide the government with sequential opportunities to ensure goal attainment by encouraging, and/or authorizing timely corrective action in those cases where results are falling short of expectations. Frequently, the accountable officials will find it necessary to assign additional assistance to lagging activities, drawing on the unallocated work hours provided for such contingencies. Where lagging results reflect deficient intra- and inter- agency collaboration, also a common occurrence, corrective action will probably require the active intervention and assistance of accountable officials. Additionally, performance reviews tend to pinpoint recurring productivity problems - problems which can only be solved by systemic changes in assignments and/or operating procedures.

Experience indicates, however, that productivity improvements are far easier to identify than to implement. In this regard, jurisdictions with specialized management improvement staffs should require their participation in performance reviews. Obviously, to do so effectively requires that they cannot rely on an ineffective study-and-report" methodology, but must forsake the diagnostic-prescriptive approach in favor of program officer education and technical assistance, working within a periodic performance review system. By working closely with program officials within a periodic reporting cycle, management improvement personnel can work on an agenda established by program officials, giving them a strong institutional base for the implementation of productivity improvements.

Work plans should incorporate performance ratios, or work standards, whenever possible. Indeed, unit measures, such as, unit cost, units per cost, output per work hour or work hours per unit of output provide the very strongest foundation for work plans. Work time forms the strongest foundation for work plans. Work time can be calculated by hour, week, month or year. As it reflects time-on-task, work time embraces all forms of effort, regardless of payment concept, including that of staff, whether permanent, part-time or temporary, overtime contributions, and time of contractors, if used. In contrast, paid time forms the basis of budgets. Thus, at the bottom of every work plan, these two different concepts are reconciled with the addition of a calculation of "authorized absences." This usually includes vacation leave, sick leave, holiday pay, etc.

Manpower planning is an integral part of the budget formulation process, especially in results-oriented budgeting which requires the

VIII. IMPLEMENTATION METHODOLOGY: DYNAMIC MONITORING

composition of work plans based on work hours. The formulation of performance targets and the composition of associated work plans based on work time effectively determine manpower requirements prior to the start of the fiscal year. It is work plans which justify proposed allocations of staff and funding.

During budget implementation, following periodic performance reviews, allotments are awarded to supervisors based on acceptance of their work plans for the ensuing period. Of course, the financial position of the government may require budget adjustment during the fiscal year. In that case, performance targets and the associated work plans should be adjusted prior to adjusting allocations. This same sequence of action should govern the work of budget officers when adjusting budget requests from program officials during the budget formulation period. Results-oriented budgets are based on targets and associated work plans. Consequently, expenditure modifications must be preceded by modification of performance targets and associated work plans, including manpower.

EXHIBIT 8.3 Work Plan: A Chief Financial Officer

ACTIVITIES/TASKS	Indicator	Q1	Q2	Q3	Q4	Total
1 **Fiscal Policy Formulation**	Work Hurs	410	320	320	365	1415
Annual Financial Report	Document	D+30				
Annual Strategic Plan	Advice		D+180			
Budget Call	Draft			D+210		
Multiyear Capital Program	Advice				D+315	
Annual Budget	Advice				D+315	
2 **Systems Development**	Work Hours	140	90	45	45	320
Improve Accounting Accuracy	Tests	D+30				
Reduce Processing Lags	Tests		D+60			
Improve Collection Ratios	Tests	D+30				
Organization Development	Sessions	DTBD	DTBD	DTBD	DTBD	
3 **General Administration**	Work Hours	280	325	375	325	1305
Finance Department Budget	Document			D+270		
4 **Miscellaneous Tasks**	Work Hours	90	185	180	185	640
5 **Performance Reviews**	Work Hours	20	20	20	20	80
Quarterly Presentations	Corrections	D+60	D+150	D+240	D+330	
Total Work Hours		940	940	940	940	3760
Add Authorized Leave (Hours)		100	100	100	100	400
Total Paid Hours		1,040	1,040	1,040	1,040	4160

NOTES:
Including the Chief Financial Officer and a Secretary, this two-position work plan is based on a work year of 260 paid days, eight hours per day, or 2080 paid hours. Authorized absences are estimated at 25 days per position, or 200 hours (Vacation Leave, 15 days, or 120 hours and Sick Leave, 10 days, or 80 hours).
"DTBD" = Date To Be Determined.

To reinforce the critical point: Governments using results-oriented budgets should conduct formal periodic performance reviews, which require the formulation of work plans. In best practice, these reviews should be conducted two-thirds of the way through each review period, which are usually quarters of the fiscal year. This practice allows time

VIII. IMPLEMENTATION METHODOLOGY: DYNAMIC MONITORING

for corrective action to attain targets, if needed. Obviously, if work plans are based on unit costs or cost per unit of output, the process will be dependent on timely reporting of expenditure information. Regrettably, tardy reporting is an outstanding weakness of government accounting systems. Consequently, these indispensable instruments of results-oriented budgets are better based on performance ratios, such as, output per work hour, or the reverse, releasing the monitoring process from undue dependence on interim cost reports drawn from the accounting system. As noted, work time forms the basis of work plans. At this point, consult 8.3, *Work Plan: Office of a Chief Financial Officer.* Based on work hours, this plan displays data discreetly, quarter by quarter..

Allotments

Allotments are important instruments of budget direction and control. Annual appropriations represent only terminal controls. They do not provide interim checkpoints as a basis for performance feedback. Appropriation allotments can play a positive—perhaps dynamic—role in program execution because they can be made discretionary in amount and timing. It is the timing quality which makes the allotment process so valuable. By allotting portions of an appropriation for expenditure at specific times, it is possible to set up a spectrum of intermediate control points which make it more likely that significant variations from work plans will be discovered early enough for corrective action. For best results, allotments must be tied to specific performance factors, or objectives. Otherwise (and this is a common observation about allotments in many governments), the apportionment process will be merely an accounting ritual to authorize further spending. If, on the other hand, allotment decisions are preceded by consultation with program personnel about specific targets, allotments can be an effective implementation instrument.

In best practice, appropriations are allotted periodically, based on expenditure plans provided by the responsible program agencies.

Budgetary Thought for Budget Officers

Although, ultimately, allotments depend on estimates of cash availability, appropriations are supposed to fund government policies and programs over a certain time period, usually one year, secured by revenue estimates. Therefore, in theory, budgets should be emancipated from constant association with the short-term cash management problems. Unless financial officials predict a total shortfall of total estimated revenue in relation to the total of appropriations, budget officers should be free to recommend work plan allotments for periods of at least three months - such work plans to reflect the results of periodic performance reviews.

Many governments allot appropriations during the fiscal year, by month or by quarter, with quarters preferred. Allotment procedures require close collaboration between agency program managers, budget officers, accounting staff and treasury officials. Experience indicates that allotment procedures can degenerate into a rather arbitrary accounting ritual (annual appropriation divided by 4 quarters or 12 months, for example) unless allotments are related to performance review procedures, and other operating requirements, listed as follows:

- A "realistic" budget, that is, a comprehensive statement of estimated expenditures and year-end obligations balanced by a conservative revenue estimate.

- A "Cash Flow Projection" prepared and updated monthly, such statements showing available balances as well as the projected inflows of revenue (including loan proceeds) for the remainder of the financial year. This is a vehicle for the maintenance of liquidity and a stable allotment process.

- Quarterly allotment requests accompanied by expenditure projections for the remaining

VIII. IMPLEMENTATION METHODOLOGY: DYNAMIC MONITORING

quarters. By its very nature, allotment approval is subject to contingencies. However, in recommended practice, if expenditure, to date, plus the requested allotments and projections are within budget, and provided that the latest estimate of the government's year-end fund balance is positive, allotment requests should be approved. Predictability encourages program planning and performance.

- An Allotment Reservation Plan, executed in orderly fashion, conditioned by reference to cash flow projections. This Plan identifies expenditures which can be deferred to specific times later in the fiscal year, such as, equipment acquisitions, new program initiatives and inventory replenishments.

Unless they are based on work plans, allotment timing and amounts result in inefficient operations, frequent breaches in expenditure control, wastage of work time and higher than expected unit costs of operations and projects.

Corrective Action

Immediately following the conduct of a performance review, the Performance Review Committee secretariat should prepare a draft report for the committee's consideration. Addressing significant performance "shortfalls," this report should recommend corrective actions to be taken by the accountable officials of the units identified during the review as problem sources and/or sources of assistance. In general form, performance reports should outline 1) performance to-date, 2) problems encountered, 3) recommended corrective actions and, 4) performance targets for the period to be covered by allotment requests, and 4) recommended allotment(s).

The identification of the recommended "corrective action" is not always easy. The term itself is an abstraction covering a variety of actions which might be appropriate in given situations. Then too, not all production problems are immediately solvable. As earlier noted, productivity improvements are far easier to identify than to implement. In many cases, the action to be recommended is rather like a 'band-aid," rather than a genuine problem resolution. Frequently, reviews pinpoint recurring productivity problems - problems which require systemic changes in operating procedures, cost center by cost center. As emphasized, representatives of key staff units, especially planning, budget, management research, human resources (personnel), and relevant centralized auxiliary service units, are expected to participate in these periodic reviews to help agency managers remove the causes of recurring production problems.

As noted above, serious implementation problems of results-oriented budgeting can be addressed by adopting and using a series of inter-related administrative practices. The following discussion reviews recommended administrative determinants and instruments.

Key Determinants and Instruments Re-Emphasized

Passing in review, the key determinants and instruments of dynamic monitoring are 1) effective articulation and use of performance information; 2) an elaborate, flexible classification and coding scheme; 3) administrative and accounting procedures facilitating the aggregation of non-monetary performance data, formally correlated with measures of effort and monetary data; and 4) continuous management utilization of four inter-related instruments of budget implementation. These instruments include a) work plans, b) allotments, c) formal, periodic "before-the-fact" performance reviews and d) timely corrective action. Effective budgeting (efficient attainment of performance objectives) is

VIII. IMPLEMENTATION METHODOLOGY: DYNAMIC MONITORING

best assured by using an institutional framework integrating these determinants, with accounting procedures providing the glue. A cautionary note concludes our discussion of budget implementation: As these determinants are mutually reinforcing, the absence or limp implementation of one reduces the effectiveness of the others.

A CONCLUDING NOTE

The strands of this book can best be brought together, and reinforced, with comments concerning the education of budget officers.

Without doubt, all budget officers are well educated, with an unknown, but substantial, proportion graduated from schools of public affairs/administration. (PA/A). A few decades ago, the typical curriculum of PA/A schools rested on a relatively sharp image of the public administrator as a non-partisan "manager," working within political environments to advance the values of effectiveness, efficiency and economy — the efficacy triad. The blurring of this image tracks to the influential 1968 Minnowbrook Conference. The conferees questioned its relevance as the key ground for PA/A curriculum. In the years since, as the image of the non-partisan manager faded, PA/A faculties offered diverse coursework justified by multi-dimensional images of public administrators, who were as likely to be engaged in policy-formulation as management.

In passing, it is worth noting that the initial PA/A school faculties drew inspiration from the government reform movements active in the early decades of the 20th century. The rather evangelical fervor of the PA/A schools evaporated after the Minnowbrook Conference. This was a price paid for loosening the organic connection between the PA/A schools and the government reform movement. Curriculum coherence inevitably suffered with the decline in faculty belief in the non-partisan manager model. However, coursework related to public budgeting remained an important curriculum component, with solid connections to specific job requirements. Indeed, in certain respects, budget officers can (and should) be thought of as prototypical public administrators, that is, the desired traits of budget officers (critical thinking, mathematical competence and affective neutrality) are desirable traits sought in all public administrators.

Thus, although concentrating on the educational requirements of a singular civil service occupation, my scope is ambitious, embracing pedagogical considerations thought to benefit public administrators generally. In that sense, a syllabus for the education of budget officers would be similarly beneficial for all public administrators. The graduate schools preparing students for government service offer courses in public budgeting mainly centered on the problems and procedures of general fund, or operating, budgets. When offered, additional courses in capital budgeting and policy analysis especially benefit prospective budget officers as they stress scholarship (critical thinking) and mathematical competence. Although not all PA/A students go on to become career budget officers, I dare to suggest that all public administration students, regardless of their future roles, would benefit if budgeting courses are designed as though all students are to become budget officers. Without diminishing the benefits to all students, this focus would ensure that those students who do become budget officers get solid academic grounding.

In sharp contrast to personal and household budgeting, the public budgeting process requires accountable officials to ration "other people's money" — a situation freighted with sundry political, economic and fiduciary implications. Obviously, budget officers are not alone among officials participating in the budget process who must take sides in the conflict between programmatic and financial values. However, as I pointed out at the beginning of this commentary, none are as continuously occupied as budget officers with providing *critical judgments* about the ways and means of spending other people's money. Although budgetary thought is by no means confined to budget officers, it is *the* preoccupation of their occupation.

Whether located in programmatic agencies, central finance units, chief executive offices or legislatures, budget officers are strategically

A CONCLUDING NOTE

placed officials whose persona and mentality are challenged by their daily struggle with the key problem facing the governments they serve: *the necessity to ration relatively scarce resources.* Their employment is undoubtedly a response to deep running socio-economic currents affecting the organization and activity of contemporary governments. Recruited and retained to 1) *assess the intrinsic merit of proposed allocations*, and 2) *assess the relative merit of all proposed claims against available resources,* their reasoned advice concerning the merit of proposed allocations should rest on criteria testing proposed programs and projects for effectiveness, efficiency and economy — the efficacy triad.

Contributing to official thinking about such considerations requires that budget officers possess appropriate mental fitness. Obviously, the requisite knowledge, skill and mental disposition have implications for the academic preparation sought in recruits, and their subsequent experience when on the job. The required mental fitness rests on a tripod comprising 1) appropriate academic attainment, 2) lessons drawn from pertinent on-the-job experience, and 3) continuing formal education in useful subjects, tools and techniques. Syllabi for the graduate and continuing education of budgetary craftsmen may embrace a variety of resources, including lectures, readings, cases, exercises, simulations, field investigations, and "mentored" internships. *Such syllabi should aim at developing scholarly skills to deal reflectively with values and computational skills to deal accurately with numbers.*

Budget work has attracted people of diverse educational backgrounds. Students of public administration, business, finance, economics, accountancy and other disciplines have found their hearth and altar in budget work. Clearly, students of public administration and public affairs have the best chance of arriving on the job with appreciation for the ways and means of public budgeting, although the pertinent course work varies in breadth and depth from school to school. Also, students of finance, business, and especially, economics, come to budget work with pertinent analytical skills. The requirement for critical thinking and clear expression favors liberal arts students.

However, whatever their academic experience, budget officers, once recruited, need, and receive, some form of "on-the-job training." The on-the job training concept should extend beyond instruction in office practice to provide systematic continuing technical and academic education of budget officers. Anything less represents an unsatisfactory state of affairs from a pedagogical point of view. Regarding the critical role of in-service education, budget officer supervisors and budget officers are advised to stress skill development and, equally important, subject-matter competence in the programmatic concerns of the jurisdiction.

Most assuredly, "critical thinking" is the most important mental instrument of budget officers. This term has a variety of interpretations. Put in scholarly terms, the phrase describes "the proper disposition for minds seeking truth." Critical thinking is the supreme skill of budget officers because they are continually confronted by the efforts of interested parties pressing claims on the public treasury. Critical thinking can be taught and learned. How best to inculcate and continually support this mental disposition? Most assuredly, the prime responsibility for cultivating this most valuable mental disposition falls to academia, considered as a truth-seeking institution. Of course, diverse faculties share this responsibility. However, professors teaching prospective budget officers must not assume that their charges have somehow acquired the habit of critical thinking during their higher learning experience. They must explicitly teach it.

On this vital point, drawing on my experience, I feel emboldened to offer specific advice on pedagogical method: Teachers of budgeting should consider adopting the time-tested pedagogical approach known in shorthand as the SQ3R Method (Credited to Francis P. Robinson, 1946). Briefly defined, this method requires 1) synoptic **S**urveys establishing configurations and relationships (the gestalt), 2) active **Q**uestioning, and 3) assiduous application of standard mental procedures facilitating comprehension and remembrance: **R**eading, **R**ecitation and **R**eview. As the concepts of survey and questioning are essential instruments of critical

A CONCLUDING NOTE

thinking, the SQ3R methodology, itself, should be taught as the initial component of budget coursework.

After attaining an understanding of the SQ3R concept, students should proceed with a survey of public budgeting, identifying patterns (e.g., executive budget formulation), design features (e.g., alternative budget formats), arrangements (e.g., legislative subject matter budget committees), and relationships (e.g., expenditures balanced to revenues). To have the desired effect on subsequent learning, students should acquire a synoptic perspective quickly, requiring an immediate scan of texts and a heavy initial reading schedule. The search for principles and patterns is very important as they transcend the ethos and practice of particular jurisdictions. Discovery of principles and patterns provides a general perspective on public budgeting, endowing observed official and interest group budgetary strivings with significance. Active questioning is the second step of the SQ3R Method. Responding to lectures, readings and cases, students should be required to compose essays addressed to significant, provocative questions, such as:

a) What is a "good" budget?

b) What is a "good" budget system and process?

c) What should a budget officer know and be able to do?

d) What is an appropriate job philosophy, or professional ethos of budget officers?

In responding to the first two questions, students are expected to identify their criteria. Also these two questions can be used to encourage students to explore the important issue of technical neutrality. Put as a query: To what extent, if any, do budget formats and procedures influence budget decisions?

Students should be encouraged to establish files (or at least notebook sections), to record ideas and information addressing questions. Provocative questions stimulate students to mine the content of lectures, readings and cases, as assigned. Essay composition encourages purposeful reflection, the practice of scholarship, and class discussions. Essays also provide a basis for grading and professorial "feedback," calculated to enhance student comprehension and performance. If cases have been assigned, student output may take the form of essays on the application of principles (or lack thereof) in the case situation. If the student is also an active civil servant or budget officer, experience-based case composition can be required, providing other students with illuminating practical insights.

The final component of the suggested academic syllabus requires field work with an accessible government, evaluating actual programmatic budgets (health, education, public safety, etc). It is especially important to provide students with an opportunity to apply criteria in appraising the quality of budget documentation and budget allocations. In addition to interviewing accountable officials, students will need access to the documentation related to 1) administrative budget formulation, and 2) the documentation provided to legislators and citizens for budget consideration and adoption.

In preparation for the field work, students should build an appraisal model, listing their evaluation criteria as queries. To the point, does the formulation documentation 1) define the issues, problems and opportunities to be attacked programmatically; 2) state goals in practical, measurable, time-bound terms; 3) identify collaborators and affected parties; 4) identify conditions required for goal attainment; 5) reference written work plans for executing the preferred programmatic solution(s); 6) display budget allocations in a programmatic (rather than commodity) format; and 7) identify alternatives considered, but rejected, and why? In Part Five, I defined the elements of the suggested appraisal model.

The suggested appraisal model puts a premium on critical thinking, emphasizing the use of evidence and logic in problem analysis, goal

A CONCLUDING NOTE

specification, the evaluation of program impact or results, and the analysis of expenditure, workload and revenue relationships. However, as the quality of budgetary thought and practice varies significantly by jurisdiction, students, by the "luck of the draw." may find themselves working with jurisdictions with less than ideal formulation and documentation standards. Given the likelihood that students may be disappointed (and perhaps disillusioned) by what they discover about government budgeting via their field work, it is important that they be taught that the purpose of the field work is the development of their critical judgment and the value of scholarship in budget work.

In their field work with subject governments, students should seek to determine the rationale used to justify expenditure allocations. As noted, a budget officer's key task is two-fold: 1) *assess the intrinsic merit of proposed allocations*, and 2) *assess the relative merit of all proposed claims against available resources.* In this connection, V. O. Key's well-known statement on this vital point may be justly quoted: "On what basis shall it be decided to allocate X dollars to activity A instead of activity B?" As with formulation documentation, students will need help in building an appraisal model to facilitate their search for allocation criteria. Exhibit 7.1 provides a suggested catalog of allocation criteria

In their field work, students will surely find most allocations justified by reference to pragmatic criteria, especially inertia, reflecting the power of programmatic and bureaucratic continuities. Throughout all levels of government, the proportion of expenditure justified by reference to formal, objective criteria is usually very small. Routinely, programs are continued from year to year, without serious reviews that apply objectives tests of effectiveness, efficiency or economy. Consequently, as previously noted, budget officers are challenged *to expand the influence of objective tests of merit in the budget process.*

Field work experiences provide a solid basis for classroom instruction regarding the importance of 1) continuous rationalization of allocation patterns by evaluating relationships between input and output/outcome/impact indicators and 2) redirecting allocations from ineffective and/or inefficient programs to new initiatives so governments can address new problems without additional taxes or loans. Required reports concerning field work experiences provide prime material for course-ending student presentations and discussions.

To deepen and broaden their thinking over the course of their careers, budget officers should continue their education in useful subjects, tools and techniques. Various media are available to enhance subject-matter knowledge, reinforce the habits of scholarship and improve computational proficiency. Institutions of higher learning, especially the PA/A schools, are likely sources for advice and assistance concerning continuing education needs and offerings. (In this respect, the availability of "on-line, remote learning" has substantially removed the impediments of time, travel and expense to continuing education.) Further, this injunction is applicable to all officials working in any given jurisdiction. Program agencies invariably employ specialists who received their formal education years before, and who have failed to keep up with changes in their field. Budget officers can help to combat this serious problem by supporting arrangements and allocations for the continuing education of program staffs. This support should be an integral component of a budget policy to encourage and support programmatic and procedural innovation.

The in-service syllabus should concentrate on analytic skill development and, equally important, subject-matter competence in the programmatic concerns of the jurisdiction. Budget officers and their supervisors share responsibility to establish and implement a syllabus with both technical and academic components, tailored to particular circumstances and perceived knowledge and skill deficits. Once thoroughly mastered, the technical aspects of budget analysis need little pedagogic attention, as practice is sufficient to maintain proficiency. In contrast, the subject-matter competence of budget officers must be an enduring supervisory concern.

Supervisors cannot assume that newly recruited budget officers have appropriate work habits and skills, especially skills related to the

A CONCLUDING NOTE

mathematical aspects of the job. Budget officers must handle numbers accurately by using techniques of control during data transfers, aggregation processes, research projects, and report preparation and presentation. This means mastering such practices as "proving" calculations, spread-sheet displays, plus and minus controls, batching to isolate error, proof-reading, making changes at the lowest level of aggregation, following strict rules for rounding, etc. The use of computer technology has greatly reduced the probability of calculation errors, and increased the ease of data aggregation and manipulation, but offer no insurance against sloppy data handling. In this connection, the phrase, "garbage–in, garbage-out" comes readily to mind. Because expenditure and revenue proposals are so often based on numerical relationships, the budget officer needs to master the techniques of statistical inference and mathematical modeling. This last point needs reemphasis as mathematical modeling offers many advantages to government officials willing to use correlations to inform budget allocation decisions.

Most important, supervisors must make sure that budget officers habitually practice critical thinking. They must handle values reflectively by using techniques of scholarship, i.e., evidence and logic. "Scholarship" normally results in systematic knowledge, that is, knowledge based on 1) an adequate, reliable assembly of information, (based on the crucial techniques of literature search and field inspection), 2) scrupulous regard for sources, 3) judicious weighing of the evidence, and 4) conclusions drawn by means of clear, consistent, and cogent reasoning. In cutting through the ambiguities of public budgeting, an econometric cast of mind is certainly an asset. If budget officers do not display this indispensable mental disposition on-the-job, it must be taught and learned as the basic qualification for continued employment. It can be truly said that, "A budget officer serving a government of general jurisdiction participates in all art and all science." To be sure, at any given time, the academic components of a budget officer's in-service education program will necessarily vary according to the programmatic agencies assigned. In addition to formal courses in relevant subject-matter, the academic in-service syllabus should include a strong program of agency field visits and library research.

The importance of the thematic content on-the-job experience in the development of effective budget officers cannot be overstated, nor should the impediments to development be underestimated. To achieve the desired enhancements in competence, the work time of budget officers must be strictly programmed. (Daily administrative tasks which tie budget officers to their desks are the chief impediments to enhancing their knowledge and skill.) On principle, the work time of budget officers should be allocated three ways: 1/3 desk-time, including budget formulation and documentation; 1/3 programmatic interaction, including field trips and dynamic performance monitoring; and 1/3 decision-related programmatic research. Also, on principle, budget officers should be sequentially assigned to different programmatic sectors to broaden their subject matter knowledge. This assignment strategy helps budget officers gain and maintain a comprehensive view of multi-sector programs and their inter-relationships. To the same end, assignment plans may include brief deployments to work in program agencies. Usually, budget officers who regularly visit the work sites and staff of assigned program agencies are significantly affected by what they see and hear. Site visits permit them to become better acquainted with the scientific-technical basis of government programs and their nomenclature. Equally important, site visits provide opportunities to observe and evaluate the conditions of work in program agency environments.

By any measure, ethics are a problematic aspect of a budget officer's persona and disposition. The willingness to stand and resist pressure is a precious, but fragile, aspect of character at all times and places, especially in bureaucratic environments. Professors who teach budgeting courses have a fundamental responsibility to acquaint their students with the ethical dimensions of budget work — to instill steel in their spines, so to speak. This is not to slight the duty of supervisors of budget officers to be sources of moral inspiration, but their role can not be specified with the same degree of certainty of force and effect.

A CONCLUDING NOTE

(Author's aside: My university mentor, Karl Bosworth, explicitly taught that the expected ethical behavior of civil servants was founded on the "willingness to resign," and frankly prescribed personal rules to that effect. My early supervisors also emphasized the moral dimensions of my work as a budget officer. Although the evidence for the influence of professors on the future conduct of students is only anecdotal, the opportunity exists, and should be eagerly seized because of the seriousness of the issue.)

In addition to consideration of the "don'ts" of ethical conduct, discussions about deportment should note positive dispositions that characterize effective budget officers. Chief among these are persistence (determination) and equanimity. Equanimity is prized as this trait helps to maintain a) decorum in situations fraught with emotion and, b) optimism in the face of inevitable disappointments when recommendations are summarily rejected, or severely compromised. One may say that budget officers should seldom utter a discouraging word, especially in interactions with program officials. Persistence is also a prized virtue. Working in environments charged with purely political considerations, budget officers frequently find that time and changed circumstances provide them with opportunities to effect recommendations once scorned. Unquestionably, the budget officer's research agenda is the prime vehicle for the expression of persistent interest in significant questions about program effectiveness, efficiency and economy.

PA/A schools are honor-bound to provide an educational experience which helps students to develop an overall orientation, or professional point of view. At an appropriate time during their academic experience, PA/A students should be asked to consider the ethical demands of administrative office in relation to their own character, mental habits and ambition. Can one be truly professional in administrative environments? After all, bureaucratic formations are widely understood to be relatively inflexible, rife with hypocrisy and typically fail to satisfy the criteria of the efficacy triad. For those who may envision becoming budget officers, the question can be made specific: "What is an appropriate job philosophy, or professional ethos, for budgetary officers?" Students assigned to draft essays on this vital subject will probably find the task difficult, and, possibly, unsettling.

It is fitting that I close this book with a note about the high calling of public administrators, in general, and budget officers in particular. In representative republics, "attaining democratically determined ends by making government work" is a responsibility of public administrators committed to constitutional means of attainment. Sad to say, many budget officers pursue a de facto philosophy of penny- pinching conservatism, cynically attacking all program values and relentlessly grasping unencumbered balances with the zeal of wartime hoarders. But neither is an attitude of free-spending liberalism appropriate for budget officers. Rather, the ideal budget officer combines a healthy respect for programmatic values (implying a sympathetic regard for the grand ends of democratic political and social life) with the tempered critical judgments of a scholar — judgments based on cultural depth and scientific understanding. Put succinctly:

A "good" budget officer is a qualified, upright judge of the worth of things.

www.ingramcontent.com/pod-product-compliance
Lightning Source LLC
Chambersburg PA
CBHW051640170526
45167CB00001B/267